Kitchen Antiques
1790 – 1940

Kathryn McNerney

COLLECTOR BOOKS
A Division of Schroeder Publishing Co., Inc.

The current values in this book should be used only as a guide. They are not intended to set prices, which vary from one section of the country to another. Auction prices as well as dealer prices vary greatly and are affected by condition as well as demand. Neither the author nor the publisher assumes responsibility for any losses that might be incurred as a result of consulting this guide.

Cover items Courtesy of Rhonda Blackburn, Kay B. Smith, and Lisa Stroup.

Front Cover:
Milk delivery box, $75.00; strainers, $8.00 each; cookie cutter, $20.00; biscuit cutter, $9.00; doughnut cutter, $10.00; nutmeg grater, $45.00; blue stoneware bowl, $65.00; potato masher, $30.00; small tin scoops, $10.00 each; child's teapot, $65.00; bread board, $65.00; bread knife, $50.00; wooden bowl, $35.00; pie rack, $135.00; pie pans, $20.00–30.00 each; dough prints, $225.00 each; stacking dry measures, $165.00 set; stoneware jar, $55.00; cookie print roller, $60.00; child's ice box, $165.00; child's kitchen items, $8.00–$15.00 each.

Back cover:
Brown stoneware bowl, $45.00; butter mold, $185.00–$225.00; measuring cups, $12.00 set; potato ricer, $25.00; standing graters, $20.00–$25.00 each; utensils, $10.00–$12.00 each; tin cup, $8.00; dry measures, $165.00 set; coffee grinder, $125.00; clown chocolate mold, $145.00; washboard, $45.00; 2 gallon crock, $125.00; large rolling pin, $95.00.

COLLECTOR BOOKS
P.O. Box 3009
Paducah, Kentucky 42002-3009

Copyright © 1991 by Kathryn McNerney

Dedicated

To You . . . Who enjoy Heritage

and

To the following . . . With my
enduring gratitude for
helping this book grow:

———————◆———————

Florida	Asbury Park	Carol Schofield
	Fernandina Beach	Eight Flags Mall; Rosanna R. Oliver
	Green Cove Springs	The Clay County Historical Museum
	Jacksonville	The Lamp Post Antiques, Inc., The Lamp Post Antiques Mall
	Mandarin	Bayard Country Store
	Middleburg	Brian and Shelly Tebo
		Jean and Chuck Stivers
		Frances and Bob Lynch
		Martha Ann McNerney
	Orange Park	Olde Town Antiques
		Timely Treasures Antiques
Georgia	Cave Spring	Cave Spring Antiques
		Country Roads Antique Mall
		Jean Walker
		Kathleen Pruitt
	Rome	Geye Hamby
		Ozment Antique Gallery
		Steven and Joan Fellows
Idaho	Kimberly	Helen Berline
		Otis Major
Illinois	Cairo	Magnolia Manor
	Glenview	Dr. Arnold E. Williams
Kentucky	Wickliffe	Carolyn Lane
New Hampshire	Keene	Robert and Ann Tebo
New York	Bergen	Elizabeth (Lisy) Smith
		Old Red Mill
	Grand Island	The Stinebrings
	Hilton	Helen Greguire
	Lewiston	Lexington Square
		Running Deer
	Ransomville	Wayne and Audrey Orr
	Wilson	Country Barn Shop
		The Tordoffs
	Youngstown	Gretchen Greene
		Old Fort Niagara Association
		Sharon Fisher
Ohio	Mansfield	The Shingle Horse
	St. Paris	Mrs. Pheobe Arnold
Tennessee	Murfreesboro	Marie's Antiques

Abbreviations

Bd	Board
BD	Base diameter
Ca	Circa, about, around the time of
D	Diameter
DP	Deep
Ea	Each
Emb	Embossed
Galv	Galvanized
Gr	Granite
H	Height
Hdle	Handle
Impr	Impressed, imprinted
Lge	Large
L	Length
Pc	Piece
Pr	Pair
Ptd	Painted
TD	Top Diameter
W	Width

Granite means graniteware
Wire means wireware
Wood means woodenware

The values listed in this book are determined by collector-owners and as shown on dealers' sales price tags. All were influenced, as always, by regional immediate buyers' activities, merchandising costs in shops, malls, and at auctions, travel and transportation expenses in searching for quality items, and the popular trends that surge and diminish in most categories from time to time.

N.P.A. denotes No Price Available.

Contents

What Goes Around

The word "kitchen" is thought to have been eventually derived from "Cycene" or one of its forms noticed in Old English (Anglo Saxon) manuscripts covering about 500 years. Ancestry regarded kitchens for cooking and cooking for living to automatically "go together," (if they ever thought about it at all.) Then once upon a time kitchens and cooking began to emerge with lengthening strides into our active awareness, their vital places in the refinements of human cultures finally recognized.

As the hands of time kept going around, early fires, habits and tools of cookery, long obscured in antiquity, similarly moved forward, each year's changes and progressions becoming clearer to historians. Advancing indoors at the Middle Ages, fires were first built on center floors of one-room shelters known as "halls," comfortable among the affluent, much less so among poor folks. With the advent of chimneys, side walls became their hearths (construction undoubtedly prodded along by discontented mutterings of growing families and overcrowding of goods stashed in such a limited space.)

Monasteries enjoyed the finest kitchens, established in separate buildings, "kitcheners" the cooks. From ancient days Northern Europeans used indoor stove devices . . . but only for heating. Cooking over open fires, baking and roasting in ovens (clay, brick, etc.) remained outside chores.

Basic cookery equipment for fireplaces was essential, easier for the housewife if more utensils could be afforded. At their forges, American blacksmiths and other metal workers preferred filling orders to a customer's fireplace measurements. Wrought iron pieces were quite simply patterned as compared to those elaborately designed in other countries. Long-handled utensils enabled cooks to stand farther back from the flames while stirring, testing, and tasting foods bubbling in kettles hung from adjustable trammels, or while basting sizzling chunks of meats being broiled. Twisted open-ringed handles on shorter helpers were to give lower heat conductivity. Strong iron chains, stationary and pivoting extension cranes at the sides or ceilings of fireplaces also held food cooking while bail-suspended in open or tightly-lidded kitchenware. Andirons (fire dogs) were in common usage in Europe in the 1400's. Used in pairs, a vertical shaft had an attached low horizontal bar to support logs for burning. Spit dogs with looped tops or hooks on the uprights held between them (crosswise) an iron rod where containers could be hung, or this could be used for broiling. All this was done over softly glowing coals raked forward onto the hearth. Here, too, leggy spiders (iron skillets) were set for baking puddings, pone, all sorts of mouthwatering smells leaking out. Within a limited radius, in cold weather, fireplaces gave off an awful lot of heat . . . in hot weather . . . likewise!

When Colonials and restless on-moving settlers first arrived in this country, they retained a familiar homeland custom for "getting started." This was for a one-room dwelling, aggravated perhaps, by urgencies of getting their families under cover, and the horrendously hard labors of erecting even that much space. And so, while a kitchen then, as always, did define "a place to prepare foods," a home still reflected the cluttered room of Medieval days.

Concentrating on as large a fireplace as possible, the room accommodated not only cookery (and smoke) but the 24-hour-a-day existence, along with paraphernalia for sewing, spinning, weaving, churning, making jams, jellies, preserves, pickles, baskets, candles, ad infinitum. During inclement weather, new leather harnesses might be made, old ones repaired, and tools sharpened. At first, without barns or sheds for storing their limited field pieces, settlers often brought in, temporarily, a small plow for instance. (All this was just great for the harried housewife crawling around and stepping over everything while trying to get a meal under way!) And there was more . . . happily if a granddad was available, he'd clear out a corner wherein to set a stool and handshell corn for meal grinding and/or soaking into hominy, crack nuts and pick out the kernels (maybe for butternut cakes), resole cherished store-bought boots, even make somewhat clumsy (sometimes the only) shoes for little ones from hides he'd cured himself. Best of all, earning heartfelt feminine gratitude – and a larger chunk of gingerbread at supper – he'd regularly hone sharper edges on steadily hard-used kitchen knives! Often there were kettle dents to be pounded out.

Early homemakers with memories of handed-down recipes (also known as receipts) for generations now revised them to the kinds of edibles found in native American fields, woods, planted gardens, streams, and at salt licks. Sweetenings might be found in "bee" trees the bears of the region also patronized. In northern climates, sap from sugarmaples was cooked into welcome syrups; farther south, cane was converted into sorghum and blackstrap molasses. Roots, herbs, barks from trees and shrubs, leaves and flowers in the forests for the taking were ingredients for dyes, flavorings, medicines, and unguents. From the room's big overhead beams, frugal cooks hung strings of beans drying for winter consumption along with pods of peppers mainly intended as autumn sausage-making seasonings. Everthing was carefully ragstrip-tied in cloth bags, away from rodents scuttling over rafters at night and flies and other insects they couldn't keep out at any time.

After awhile, when time and purse permitted, lofts were floored for sleeping pallets, also commandeered by wives for drying apples and other foods. Extended pantries held "canned" – to use one word to cover all the ways of "putting by" – foods as well as kitchenware only occasionally needed; ells and sheds received all other objects crammed into the kitchen unrelated to its primary function – cooking.

Widely – and wildly – acclaimed by American manufacturers when coal/wood burning stoves appeared circa 1830, public acceptance was equally enthusiastic. The word "range," of Teutonic origin, meaning herein a row or series of openings (wells) over fires, generally became "cookstove" or merely "stove" by the mid-1800's. (Made in China, a cast iron stove was found dating back to circa 200 A.D.) In the United States, with iron foundries increasing circa 1724, "Dutch" stoves of five plates were sold by circa 1728. With the excitement of stoves "standing free of walls," certain models could be used for either or both cooking and heating. There were grates and sliding door base burners for coal and/or wood among many other progressing features. Original stoves can still be found with diligent searching among shops, auctions, flea markets, and advertisements of private owners. An old one is difficult to precisely evaluate; condition and repairs/replacement parts are to be considered,

proximity and costs of securing wood for burning, and transporting the heavy iron. Finally, its worth seems important only to those wanting to actually use it and/or seeking the popular "country look." (Many declare nothing tastes as deliciously different as foods prepared on an old cookstove.)

Original wrought utensils of iron, brass, copper, pewter, et al., made by smithies, tinners, coopers, and so on, do exist in small numbers; but largely, for years when a helper became severely worn, bent, or its handle beyond fixing, the piece was just tossed out.

With the innovation of stoves saving time and energies for cooks, kitchenwares also entered a new field. As with craftsmen's tools, those that had always been durable, practical, and easy to store and use survived, such features continuing. Manufacturers began to produce in quantities with slight or drastic changes and improvements, steadily adding a multitude of entirely new gadgets with advertised advantages.

Kitchens changed without noticeable pauses from small to roomy to galley into the 1900's, decorators eventually deciding on an all-white decor, kitchenwares of many materials and forms aping that (now considered) rather dull theme. Handles had for so long been left in their natural wood tones, then whitened or blackened, other cookery equipment correspondingly bland. Nearing the 1920's, the spirits of earnest cooks were surely energized when a veritable rainbow evolution burst into their domains. Placid hand helpers brightened, often bought to match walls, woodwork or tiles. Apple greens, yellows, crimson reds, occasional blues, many white striped, emerged foremost on handles. (Nature builds from greens so it evidently seemed a restful kitchen color.) Other forms and materials of cooking accessories soon joined the parade. A host of gimmicks began filling up drawers, some in everyday handling, others hastily purchased as novelties, tried out several times, then stashed away as frustrating nuisances.

Recently I asked my daughter her favorite food. Without hesitation she replied, "D . . . D for Dough." Later, thinking about it, I realized that "D" does pleasantly and appetizingly occupy a large space in our culinary lives. And who among us would not – in passing – wish for a second whiff of fresh baked bread from a baker's shop, enjoy the marvelous scent of hot pies when entering a kitchen after an especially rough (maybe wintry) day, or deeply inhale when cotton seeds being pressed into oils make a whole county smell like dough-wrapped hams being sugar baked in ovens . . . who for just a moment does not experience a quick nostalgia for a kitchen once known . . . a kitchen perhaps read about . . . a kitchen dreamed of.

With its hands having ticked away another full circle, as the clock begins another round, so have kitchens traveled full-centuries' circles . . . open fires out on the ground . . . later ringed with stones . . . moving indoors into a room where cooking could be done in a fireplace . . . climbing up onto stoves . . . today's cooks utilizing both indoor and outdoor facilities. Finally, with their singular identities firmly established as "places for cooking," kitchens can again admit some of those things additionally sheltered so long ago ... like rocking chairs and other comfortable furniture welcoming families and their friends to gather together (plus a television so the cook can catch a newscast as she gets a meal under way.)

And so it is . . . kitchens are ready to go 'round again into still another century . . . for whatever that may hold.

Of Fireplaces and Stoves

Double Ovens at Bakehouse Old Fort Niagara, N.Y.

Held by the French when the bakehouse burned in 1761, restored from foundations that remained when the British held the Fort in 1762, yielded to the United States in 1796, recaptured in 1813 by the British, and ceded to the United States again in 1815. Bread for the garrisons was baked here until 1870. N.P.A.

Dough Raiser/Mixer Old Fort Niagara, N.Y.

Mixed inside the box, dough could be "worked" on the lift-off lid. 3" thick wood. 45"H., 78"L., 36"W., N.P.A.

Fireplace at "The Castle," Old Fort Niagara

Cast iron **pivoting crane** sized to small area and **footed kettle** of cast iron; wrought iron **coals tongs**. N.P.A.

Andirons

Ca. 1800s. Cast iron, 16½"H., 8½"L., $145.00.

Hearth Shovel

Ca. mid-1800s. Cast and forged iron, 22"L.; spade, 4¼"W., $25.00.

Meat Hooks

Ca. 1800s. Hand fashioned iron wire to hang on fireplace trammels and chains with chunks of meat on the points for roasting, or for suspending kettles over the coals; the sharper was probably fastened with others on a board for hams and bacons, even utensils. 6" and 7"L., $12.50.

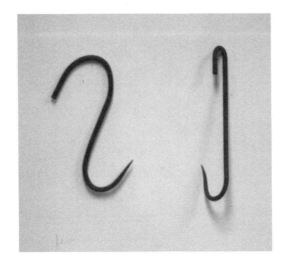

Fireplace Logs Fork

Ca. 1800s. Wrought and cast iron; twisted handle, knob top; three prongs control logs, turning and moving them about for better burning. While it could have served in a large home, it more likely stood ready at the fireside of an inn's cooking room. 42"L., $35.00.

Peel

Ca. 1840. Smithy-wrought iron whose handle widens just above the flat spade, firming it; although used for wherever needed, these shorter-handled ones are more commonly known as cake or pastry peels, bread peels the longer handled; a few (entitled to) age and wear nicks., $95.00 – 125.00.

Trivet

Ca. early 1800s. Smithy wrought iron; comfortable handholding curve; similar style made to hold pressing irons but the area here intended for general usage, the width more suitable for holding pots and pans. 10"L., $195.00.

Fender Trivets

Ca. 1890s. Blackened cast iron; each has a back protruding prong with screws to attach; one a horseshoe, the other feathery curlicues forming sides of a center solid. Both 6"H., 5½"W., $45.00.

Footman/Trivet

Ca. 1800s. Polished cast iron with ashes still adhering in the creases; gracefully curved high legs hold a teakettle or hot water jug by tableside on its prettily feathered patterned plateau. 3½"H., 8¼"W., $125.00+.

Trivets, made of iron, brass, copper, silver, silverplate, tile, even glass over metal; innumerable styles in flat-topped stands (usually three legs), were to hold hot dishes away from damage to (wood) surfaces, keep food warm at fireside and beside a table; those shaped to smaller plateaus were for pressing irons.

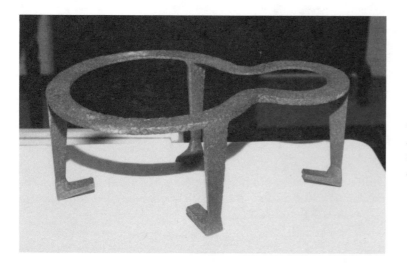

Trivet

Ca. 1700s. Wrought iron; uncommonly-shaped feet; age-worn but still in good condition; larger circle diameter is 6". 3½"H., 9"L., $87.50.

Warming Oven

Ca. 1800s. All original; seen in north central Georgia; cast iron, porcelain profiles, stamped elaborately designed metal frames for heads; the oven was bricked into the side of a fireplace; even the heat emission holes in the base are patterned in rounds and diamonds; looks like there were grooves for resting a second shelf below the top barred one; iron knobs on bowed convex doors. 18½"H., 31"W., 12½"DP., $275.00. More to area displayed.

Kitchen Range/Cookstove

Ca. 1890s – early 1900s. Cast iron, nickel; emb: GLEN-WOOD CABINET MODEL, Weir Stove Co., Taunton, Mass.; complete as original with the exception of the new stovepipe; lift-up bowed warming oven door – iron wire keeper trimmed handlehold; lid lifter seen on one stove plate; baking oven heat indicator; today, burning wood, it regularly serves in a northern farm kitchen (and I know the food is delicious for I had dinner there.) And, of course, utilitarian and decorative values are considered top criteria. 62"H., 39"W., $850.00.

Cookstove

Black cast iron, white porcelain, small nickel trim; on a brass plate is KALAMAZOO SERIES 2, ERIE; stovepipe not yet installed; hot water reservoir; two warming ovens behind lift doors; temperature indicator; four wells with lift-off plates. 60¾"H., 47"W., $815.00+.

*Beside the stove is an early handmade **pine chimney cupboard;** traces of original mustard yellow paint remain after stripping; whittled turn catch. (That's Thumper the cat who refused to get down.)*

Stove

Ca. 1800s. Cast iron; wood placed in the side box for burning; stovepipe missing but collar remains; lid lifter there to remove well plate; dropfront door and wire shelf. 25½"H., 26"W., 21"DP., $225.00.

Stove

Cast iron box style, emb: SPECIAL - (the rest is blurred); made for Sears Roebuck & Co. sales by Orr, Painter & Co. (Reading Stove Works), Reading, Pa.; heavily reproduced; long handled sheet iron **shovel** *on the wall was to remove ashes and clinkers, those slaggy coal pieces fused together and improperly burned. N.P.A.*

Toy Stove

Cast iron, porcelain; Rival, J.E. Stevens, Cromwell, Conn.; ornate overall; does successfully still burn wood; new stovepipe section on original collar; six burners; hot water tank. 13"H., 18"W., $245.00.

Stove

Cast iron, white enamel; #26 SPECIAL, emb: SOUTHERN COOPERATIVE FDRY, ROME, GA.; listed in old City Directory 1898–99. After 1887, stove manufacturing became one of Rome's largest industries, the town said to have been among the top stove producers in the United States. Southern Cooperative the last of those foundries. N.P.A.

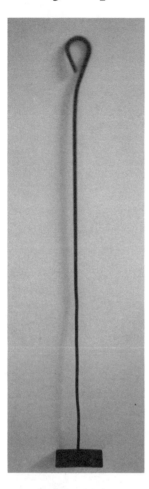

Flue Rake

Ca. 1870s. Sheet iron, wire; to reach high in stovepipes and far back in low base burners to clear out soot, clinkers, or charred bits of wood and unburned slivers of coal, even vagrant leaves and twigs blown about that blundered into the mouth of the stove's outside vent if it had no mesh for protection, $10.00.

Coals Saver

Galvanized tin, wood; sides and bottom are perforated; the long handle kept blowing grit away from one's face; picked up bits of coal not burned, those particles to be frugally reused. 42"L., $45.00.

Dampers/Stovepipe Plates

Ca. 1800s. All cast iron; valves in the flue pipes to regulate drafts by turning; two have twisted wire handles, one is solid; all are AMERICAN or NEW AMERICAN, GRISWOLD, Erie, Pa. U.S.A., one emb, one impr. 9" D. Pat. dated Apr. 30, 1880; 6" D. Pat. dated Mar. 23, 1876; 3" D. Pat. Pend. Apr. 30, 1880, $18.00 – 35.00.

Stove Well Plate

Ca. 1800s. Blackened cast iron; lacy design; lift tab, $37.50.

Coal Scuttle/Hod/Bucket

Ca. late 1800s. To cover scars, 4th generation of the same family painted over the original black japanned finish. Following the usual practice of starting a fire in the stove on a cook's early morning, before bedtime the hod was filled from an outside "woodshed" or such with small lumps of coal, slivers of kindlin', and sometimes crushed bits of paper. Lifted by its wire bail, the user tipped it against the rim of the fire well, then tilted the hod so the coal would gradually slide out the wide lip, not all going in at once to crush the slowly-glimmering blaze already begun from the paper and kindlin'. Customarily the bucket stood in a regular place, at the side and near the back of the stove, kept filled to be ready all day for the needs of the cook. 11"H., 15¾"TD., $35.00.

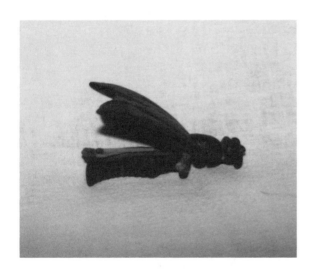

Match Holder/Box

Ca. 1800s. Black iron realistically cast as a fly. The front wings are hinged for lifting above body where matches were handily kept, these friction-lighted by striking on the ridged underside of the fly. Early matches were long, thinly-rounded wood splinters dipped in melted sulphur which hardened. Match boxes are fun to collect, take up little space, and can be found in many materials in many forms. 4¼"L., 2½"W., $75.00.

---◆---

Match Safes/Boxes

Cast iron. Both embossed on lids and have rough crisscrossing on the bottoms for striking matches.

Hinged lid below decorative box gallery. Emb: SELF CLOSING ... FOR MATCHES AND C. ... Patd. Dec 20, 1864, D M & CO, NEW HAVEN. 4"L, 2½"W., $78.00.

Dog Running Looking Back Over His Shoulder. *Foliage, dotted frame, Patd. Jan 21, 1862. 4"L, 2½"W., $85.00.*

---◆---

---◆---

Stoves' Tools

Ca. from the mid-1800s. All are black cast iron and are 7" to 9" L. except for the poker.

Coals poker. *Wire handle, 19"L., $18.00.*
Ash shaker. *Square mouth to fit over stove bar., $18.00.*
Ash shaker. *Square mouth to fit over stove bar, perforated handle. $18.00.*
Stove well plate lid lifters. *Curved with open ring wire handle, uncommon style with pronged short lifter end. $12.50.*

---◆---

Wall Oven/Stove

Ca. 1800s. Cast iron and brick. Emb. on doors: STAR RANGE, CINCINNATI, OHIO. Drop-door at back fronts a wall oven below a high warming shelf; lower iron shelf has surface open (or covered when not needed). Wells over fire to set cooking containers; can be adjusted to desired heats. On stove side hangs an uncommon square **fry skillet** *by Griswold, Erie, Pennsylvania. N.P.A.*

Pipe Tongs

Ca. 1800s. Brass, to carry a warm coal from the hearth for lighting tobacco in the clay pipes. They also carried live coals in the serrated bottom-edged tongs to start a fire in another fireplace at another location. 8¼"L., $35.00.

Pipe Box

Walnut; sliding door; leaf and flower designs; scalloped top. These held long clay pipes for the men in the family and for offering to guests. Tobacco was carefully tamped into the pipes and lighted with a taper from the fireplace. They hung, generally, close to the opening. 7¼"L., 3½"W., $135.00.

Cooking Helpers For The Hands

Utensils Rack

Ca. 1700s. Wrought in iron; many so finely designed as this one were gifts for special occasions, given by the smithy himself, or made to customers' orders. Those with wooden backs usually had iron hooks, but others had wooden pins inserted into auger-bored or burned-through holes. Utensils extend the cook's abilities, kitchen helpers that accomplish tasks those hands could never achieve alone. Contact with extreme heat and cold, slicing, reaching, chopping, to name a few ... we only begin to count their benefits. In collector parlance the words pin and peg are commonly similarly applied, to small bolt-like forms (wood or metal) for pinning boards and many other things together, as wall hangers, giant-sized ones as vent hole plugs in casks, etc. And so 'tis ... a peg is a pin and a pin is a peg. $275.00.

◆———————————————◆

Apple Parer

Ca. 1820's. Shaker, pegged maple; placed on a bench so the owner could straddle sit at the longer end; the leather wheel strap and several other parts are missing. A push-rod shoved a pared apple on past a metal plate into the box; four side blades had already cored and quartered it. Straddle seat board 24"L., 6½"W., the other board 21"L., 8"D. wheel, $375.00.

First hand cranked, later there was a spring-activated device of wood, cast iron, and a few other materials. Rotated against a blade, a speared fruit was pared, the later models coring, quartering, and slicing. They were covered by many and varied patents ca. 1840, then commerically made in large numbers. Early handcrafted examples are now choice collectibles and heritage-unique. After being laid on shed roofs, on floors of kitchen lofts, or hung from beams close to the fireplace for drying, apples were delicious in winter pies.

◆———————————————◆

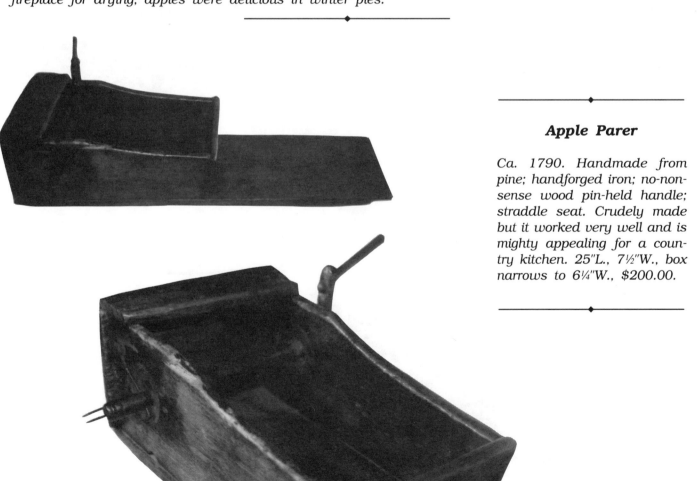

◆———————————————◆

Apple Parer

Ca. 1790. Handmade from pine; handforged iron; no-non-sense wood pin-held handle; straddle seat. Crudely made but it worked very well and is mighty appealing for a country kitchen. 25"L., 7½"W., box narrows to 6¼"W., $200.00.

◆———————————————◆

Apple Parer

Ca. early 1800's. Straddle seat; screwed to bench; dark stained maple; wooden screw controls spring-loaded parer arm to keep tension on the fruit; pewter ferrule holds tines. 19"L., 7¾"W base, 7½"D. wheel, $395.00.

Apple Parer

Ca. early 1800's. Plain and simple style in pine, maple and oak; four leather adjusting rings; leather belt is gone; pewter collar holding iron tines. 6½"H., 18½"L., $225.00.

Apple Parer

Ca. 1700's. The earliest parer among these shown; black walnut; string pulleys; smithy-forged decorated center of tines; wingnut fastened; set on a table or bench in usage. 28½"L., 7"W., 7"D. wheel, $400.00.

Apple Parer

Ca. 1850. Shaker; straddle seat; two-way boards mixed woods; wooden wheel pegs mesh into the center holes of the spindle; brass ferrule forms long forged iron apple-holding spears; simple squared handle with knob looks age and usage worn; turned sturdy legs tapering to the floor; thought was given to shaping the seat end for more straddle comfort. 16"H., 27"L., seat rounded to 7½"W., $395.00.

Apple Parer

Ca. early 1800's. Maple; straddle-bench with four turned, splayed legs for rigidity; large inside parer knife between wheel and box is steel; one revolution of the wheel turned the paring blade eight times – pared, cored, and quartered the apple; lines decorate handle; brass ferrule. 38"L., thick wheel is 14"D., $325.00.

Apple Parer

Ca. 1800. Maple; iron; leather belt driven, long tines; pewter ferrule. 32"L., 5½"W., 7"D. wheel, $175.00.

◆

Apple Parer

Ca. 1840–50. Pine, iron; curve designed one end of straddle seat; unusually long handle; pegs mesh with cogwheel in turning. 23"L., 8"W., $400.00.

◆

◆

Apple Parer

Cast iron, wood; rotary action; wingnut table fastener. Emb: '78 U.S.A. MADE ONLY BY THE READING HARDWARE CO. READING, PA. Patented March 6, 1872, Feb. 17, 1874, Oct. 19, 1875, Feb. 22, 1876, Nov. 14, 1878, and May 22, 1877. Sharp apple impaling spikes; elaborate iron castings, $80.00.

◆

Apple Parer

Ca. 1800's. Maple; leather belt driven; iron tines; pewter ferrule; straddle seat. 22"L., 5½"W., 7"D. wheel, $195.00.

Fruit Press

Ca. 1890. Solid cherry; copper; Midwest origin; fruit, such as grapes, placed in the reservoir were firmly mashed when the handle-operated plunger base plate came down inside; squeezed out the juices that flowed into containers set beneath; three base tapering, turned legs; turnings all line decorated. 33"L., $325.00.

Apple Butter Stirrer

Ca. 1870. Handmade from hickory; 40"L. mortised and braced handle; wood pinned to a stirring foot with unevenly bored holes. When heat under a plop-popping kettle of fruit made a kitchen too hot to endure, the cook might move outside, leaving the kettle in the fireplace, and reaching through (probably the only) window, stir the cooking mass with a long-handled stirrer (they came in innumerable sizes), both she and the handle leaning on the sill. $45.00+.

Apple Butter Fireplace/Yard Kettle

Ca. 1870. Rarely seen now complete with wooden mixer; copper; iron bail; rolled rim; dovetails hold side joinings and attach the separately made bottom; a metal plate securely hooks one end of the crossbar; the handle turns the post so base paddles can mix and stir; eyeholes in the paddles make this easier as thickening sauces more easily slip through. If she preferred – or in bad weather – the housewife could remove the center fixtures, hang the kettle on a heavy iron (chain) trammel, and stir its contents with a long mixer. $495.00.

Cake Turners/Spatulas

Both tin; pressure brings together wire double handles, flat spade flips over food (griddle cakes, pancakes, Niagara Frontier and New England fire cakes, eggs, and so on).

Flipper solid turner. *Curled ring handle top; the earlier of these. 12"L., $25.00.*

"Poppie" turner. *Stamped perforations in lines; holes allow grease to drip back into cooking container when lifting out the cakes. 11"L., $25.00.*

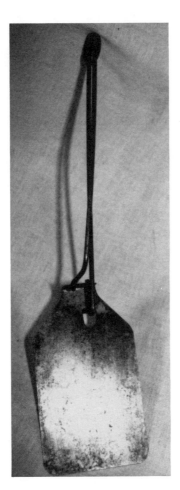

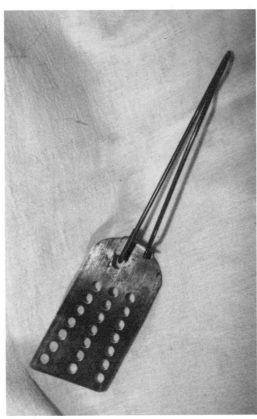

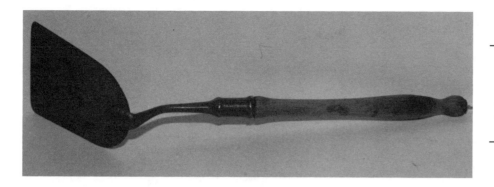

Cake Turner/Spatula

Ca. 1890. Turned wood, metal, wide collar. 14"L., $25.00.

Cookie Crimper/Marker

Ca. Late 1800s. Maple; satiny pattern turned handle; sheet tin crimper. 4½"H., 2½"D., $58.00.

Ladle/Dipper

Ca. 1700s. Handcut treenware from one piece of apple wood. 2" Deep bowl, 11½"L., $165.00.

Cup/Goblet

Ca. 1700s. Handcarved poplar; originally a smooth rim has now, through age and usage, become almost a sawtooth; an eating-table piece. 5"H., 3½" TD., $250.00+.

Biscuit/Cookie Cutters

Ca 1800s–1900s. Tin; arched rolled-edge strap handles; fairly sharp on the base cutting edges; could fit together to save storage space when not in use. 2¾"D., 2¼"D., 1½"D., $18.00 – 20.00.

Pastry Blender

Ca. 1900s. Nickeled iron; green painted wood handle. 9½"L., $18.00.

Batter Bowl

Ca. 1800s. Earthenware; outside roughly brown, inside brightly glazed; has the better-to-hold-on-to-rim; English origin. 9"H., 19"D., $75.00.

Cookery Utensils

Molds. Ca. 1900s. Gray tin, fluted skirts for jellied desserts; diamond and oval shapes; both marked A & J., $12.50 each.

Biscuit cutter. Ca. 1900s. Gray tin, rolled rim; spot-soldered squared arc handle; 3"D., 2"H., $9.00.

Doughnut cutter. Ca. 1890s. Gray tin, stamped out with fluted sides; never had a handle., $18.00.

Wide mouth canning jar funnel. Ca. 1890s. 2¼"H., 5"D., $15.00.

Tea Biscuit Cutter

Ca. 1930s. Also a cookie cutter; green painted wood handle; scallops; old ones were sometimes made by traveling tinners from scraps they'd accumulated, or they were cut by householders themselves; found in forms too numerous and varied to count. 1½"H., 2⅜"D., $7.50.

Cookie Roller

Ca. 1875. Rich patina on one of the nut woods; base shaped to press or lightly pound dough; bulb-turned handle; 10 corrugated rings with stubborn dough traces still clinging in the grooves; a few small not unexpected chips; tight handle split. 12"H., $55.00.

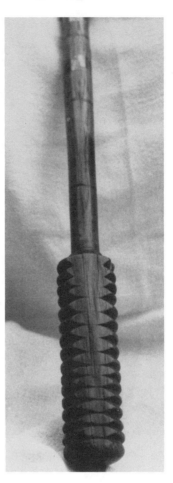

♦
Cookie Roller/Fret
♦

Ca. 1875. Walnut; 15 corrugated rings and rounded button base for pressing or gently pounding the dough; one side flat for pressing also; a few minor no-harm chips; in the same family for several generations. 14"H., $55.00.

♦
Dough Box Roller

Ca. 1890–1900s. Pine; dough placed inside box to "raise" was then kneaded down by the handle-turned roller. Much easier and quicker than kneading doughs by hand. 22"L., 8½"W., 7"DP., $165.00.
♦

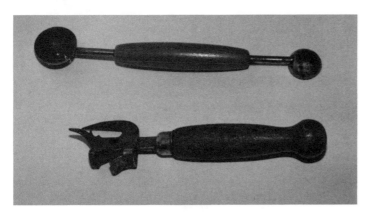

Double-End Baller/Melon Scoop

Ca. 1930s–40. Wood, stainless steel; center baller holes for excess juices of fruit to drip out; also popular for potato balls. 7⅝"H., $10.00.

Can & Cap Bottle Opener

Ca. 1915–20. Cast steel, wood, brass ferrule; A & J Diamond trademark. 6"H., $25.00.

Can & Cap Bottle Opener

Ca. early 1900s. Steel and natural wood handle. 6⅛"H., $18.00.

Can & Cap Bottle Opener

Ca. 1800s. Blackened wood square handle with steel and a metal ferrule. 6½"H., $18.00.

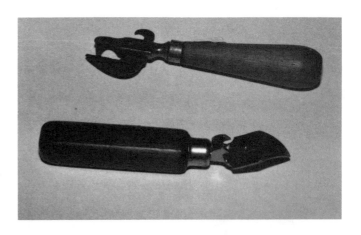

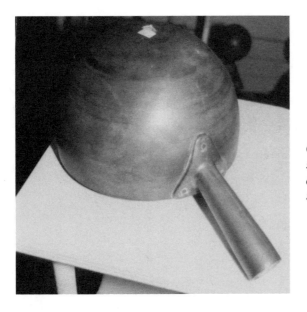

Candy Dipper

Ca. 1900. Copper, dulled by the years; Pennsylvania origin; handle riveted on and has convex closed end. 9"H., 10"TD. bowl., $78.00.

Candy Hatchet

Ca. 1900. Cast iron; to break up hard candy (peanut brittle, for instance) into convenient bite-size pieces. 8¾"L., $28.00.

Cottage Cheese Crock

Ca. 1910. C.H. BERLING, INC., BONDHILL DAIRY; filled for home use; when the bowl was emptied, could be returned for refilling; advertising printing black on white. 4¾"H., 8"D., $78.00+.

Cheese Drainer

Ca. 1800s. Shaker type; wood, twisted wire; bentwood nailed and wire stapled; very fine mesh; hanging string. 3½"H., 12"D., $58.00.

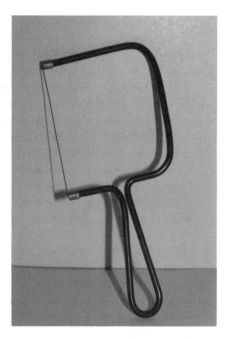

Cheese Slicer

Ca. 1920s. Iron and fine sharp wire; thin blade drawn saw-like through cheese for slicing. 6⅞"H., $18.00.

Cherry Seeder/Stoner

Ca. 1900s. Cast iron; wood; emb: ROLLMAN MFG. CO. No. 8. Only one or two were put into the hopper at a time to avoid mashing the berries; as the handle turned the cherry rubbed against the grooved plate; the stone (pit) fell out one side and the cherry the other; wingnut screws to table. 12"H., $50.00.

Cherry Seeder/Stoner

Ca. 1890. Tinned cast iron; table fastened; these were to remove seeds without crushing the fruit; emb: ENTERPRISE CHERRY STONER NO. 1; as a cherry was fed into the cup, the handle activated the shallow ridged rotary wheel, rubbing against the fruit, removing the pit. Note exit trough. 8"H., $65.00.

Choppers

Wrought iron blade; *cast tubed iron blade-width handle. Pat Feb. 1887. $48.00 – 70.00.*
Wrought iron blade; *wood grip. Ca. 1880. $45.00 – 75.00.*

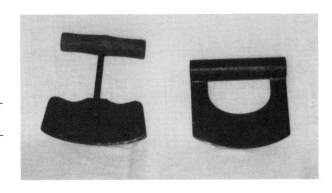

Chopping/Mincing Knives

Wishbone shaft; *wood grip; cast steel blade. Ca. 1880–1900. $45.00.*
Cast iron shaft and blade; *copper riveted together; maple handle. Ca. 1860. $65.00.*
Double tangs holding wood handle; *sausage-shaped tin blade. Ca. 1870. $58.00.*

Chopping Knife

Ca. 1880. Iron wishbone shaft, turned shaped maple grip; narrow wrought tin blades slightly askew. $75.00.

Doughnut Cutter

Ca. 1900s. Tin; wide arched handle. 2½"H., 2½"D., $18.00.

Cooks' Choppers/Mincing Knives

Ca. 1800s. All handforged iron with wood handles; second from the bottom is the oldest (ca. 1860) anchor-shaped blade. From the early 1700s into the early 1900s, choppers were single or double tangs, these attached to wood or iron handles, the latter solid or tubed; innumerable shapes, sizes, and materials in combinations. But all were used with wooden bowls, most housewives lap-holding them for knives chipping meats or vegetables, mincemeat making a seasonal specialty. $50.00 – 75.00.

Dipper
Blue and white speckled granite. 14"L., $35.00.

Turkey Basting Spoon
Speckled blue granite. 14"L., $29.00.

Civil War Field Cookery Cup
Ca. 1861-65. Tin; for heating small amounts of food over open fires and on portable stoves in field kitchens; double folded wire handle; wood lift knob. $45.00.

Coffeepot

Tin; long handle; curved tilt strap-shaped bar and lid lift; long wide spout; some had a mesh inside to hold back the coffee grounds – if no mesh, they let the grounds "settle" to the bottom – if any escaped, it was up to the drinker. Typical size for field kitchens, ranch trail wagons cookery, possibly even an early frontier inn. 10"H., 6"BD., 5½"BD., $95.00.

Coffee Mill

Ca. 1840. Cherry with chamfered top; cast iron fixtures; hand-hammered brass collar around gears cup. Mills are grinders, named by the regions; all are about the same – inside iron grinding wheels handle turned to crush the roasted beans poured into the top well. These bits drop into a pullout drawer; made of wood or various metals. The mills produce a product with a distinctive flavor that brewing enhances; today many cooks still prefer grinding their own roasted beans in one of these – or similar – old grinders. 6½" square, $225.00.

Coffee Mill

Ca. Late 1800s. Brass, cast iron. ornamental plate. WILLIAM COTTON COFFEE MILL (England). $145.00.

Coffee Mill

Wood dovetailed four corners; cast iron fixtures including inside gears; tin screw top lid; pullout drawer is of bentwood, straight front, and ring-trimmed knob. $125.00.

Coffee Mill (also known as Grinder)

Elaborately patterned cast iron, wood and brass; sliding lid over well where coffee beans are added and where iron gears are activated in grinding by turning the uncommonly long handle; pullout drawer to receive the ground beans. Along the trail of ownership, someone stove blacked the whole wood cabinet. 5¾"H., 5½" Square, $125.00.

Coffee Mill

Pressed glass jar, cast iron, wood grip; brass collar; emb: PATENT PENDING and FEB. 14, 1905; screws onto a wall, side of a cabinet, wherever space allowed and was convenient. 9¾"H., $50.00.

Corkscrew

Ca. 1800's. Realistically handcarved alligator from a deer's antler forms the handle of this piece; fixtures are steel. A cork-guide-cap fits over a bottle top, making better leverage and more assurance the cork crumbs won't fall down into the contents as when dug out with a knife point. 8"L., $275.00.

In an effort to stop invasions of insects and rodents when corks protruded above the bottle tops, they were cut flush with the top. Dating from the mid-1600's, this led to progression as well in the removal devices, especially among wine makers and bottlers. Of many materials, shapes, sizes, and a host of patents, corkscrews included folding types for carrying about in pockets and pocketbooks (purses).

Corkscrew

Ca. 1800's. Handcarved from a deer's antler, black; steel fixtures; bottle top guide cover anchors the instrument. 8"L., $275.00.

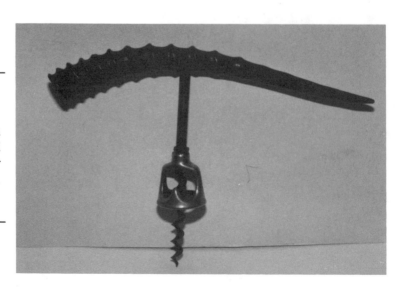

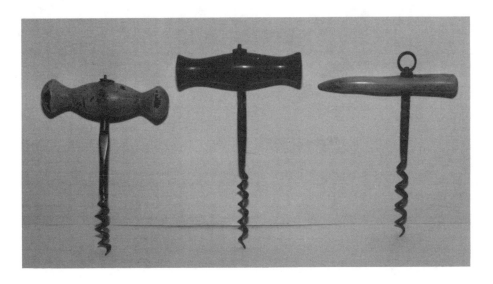

Corkscrew

Ca. late 1800s. Watermelon-shaped handle in darkened shiny wood; steel. 5"L., $45.00.

Corkscrews

Steel; chubby rosewood handle; ca. 1800s–1920s. 4½"H., $65.00.
Steel; green painted wood handle; ca. 1800s–1920s. 5½"H., $35.00.
Steel; handle made from a deer's antler; wire ring; ca. 1800s – 1920s. 4½"H., $45.00 – 55.00.

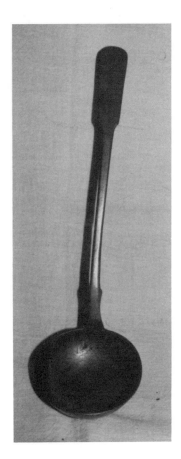

Corkscrew

Ca. 1880s. Wood, steel, brass ferrule; handle turns spiraled wire, and sharp screw point into cork; cap guide. $48.00.

Dipper

Ca. 1700s. Hand-crafted pewter; designed handle; carries the soft gleam and satiny patina of age, usage and good care. 12¼"L., 3½"D. bowl, $195.00.

Dipper

Ca. 1800s. Copper; has considerable wear but no holes; dents and a rolled rim split here and there; brass rivets attach the closed-end, tapered hollow handle. 4⅝"H., 10¾"TD., 5"L. handle, $150.00.

Egg Beater
Cast iron, tin; emb: TAPLIN'S DOVER PATTERN IMPROVED. Pat'd. Apr. 14, 1903. 12½"H., $45.00.

Egg Whisk/Whip
Ca. 1930s. Inn and baker's size wire, wood handle, 17¾"H., $18.00.

Potato Masher
Ca. early 1900s. Heavy gauge twisted and rim-wrapped oval crisscross masher wire; two sides hold wood handle. 10"H., 3½"D., $38.00.

Egg Beater
Cat iron, wood, tin; emb: TAPLIN MFG. CO. NEW BRITAIN, CONN. Pat'd. 1908. 12¼"H., $78.00.

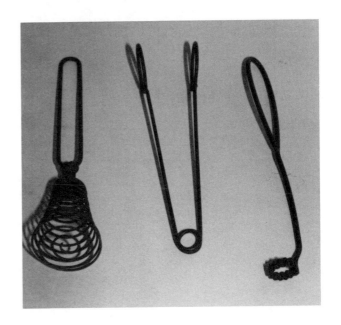

Egg Whisk/Whip

Ca. 1880s. Black tin and wire; coiled and straight. 7½"H., $15.00.

Egg Lifter

Ca. 1880s. Black tin and wire; spring action. 8½"H., $10.00.

Fritter Fryer

Ca. 1880s. That is the description the dealer gave this black tin and wire item; it might be a garnisher/shaper for fruits and vegetables, or for coring; only its first owner knew for sure. 8¾"H., $20.00.

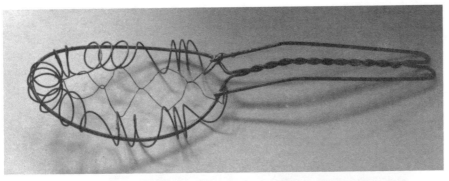

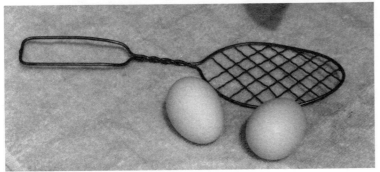

Egg Whisks/Whips

Ca. 1930s. Both tinned wire; diamond centers. Each has one piece of wire folded into whip paddle frame and handle; may have also served to whisk other light foods such as cream sauces. Double handle with center twist, 10½"L., $25.00. Single handle, 9"L., $15.00.

Scissors Lifter/Tongs

Ca. 1930s–40s. Heavy gauge metal, each end mashed into three points to lift foods from frying skillets – as chicken parts, fried vegetables, fish, etc., $18.00.

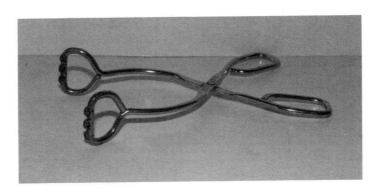

Cookery Fork

Ca. 1700s. Shaker; hand-carved from one piece of wood; three long tines; an item family-cherished for many generations with practically no wear signs. 33"L., $175.00+.

Flesh/Meat Fork

Ca. late 1800s. Tinned wrought iron; shank is brass riveted between two tapered 13" lengths of hickory handle; only one rivet remains. $28.00.

Flesh Fork

Ca. 1800s. Wire; three sharp prongs, one slightly point-bent; made from two iron wire lengths; one forms the outside tongs, looped for a handle, then was brought down to form the other tine; a second piece is at center, all held together with two metal clips. 15"L., $22.50.

Flesh Fork

Ca. 1700s. Wrought iron; to pierce food for "doneness"; very sharp tines. 17½"L., $75.00.

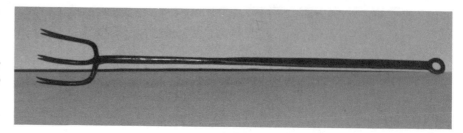

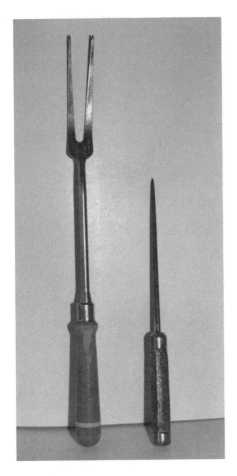

Flesh Fork

Ca. 1920s–40s. Stainless steel prongs; one end worn flat; green painted handle with white stripe; ferrule. 14½"L., $10.00.

Ice Pick

Ca. 1920s. Very heavy metal; sharp bayonet spike; chipped off bits of ice from a large chunk – delivery man first scored deep lines where he wanted the block to break when he chipped – they were experts. Often, kids gathered at the back of the wagon and he'd chip flakes their way. $25.00.

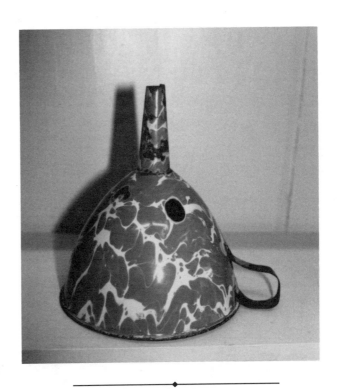

Funnel

Ca. 1880s. Bold blue and white eye-catching granite; unusual curved handle; minor wear. 9"H., 7½"TD., $45.00.

Funnel

Ca. 1800s. Tin; copper tipped; extra-large, rolled edge, comfortably including inside fingers rest handle; for filling containers such as jugs. 20"H., 7"TD., $45.00.

Funnel with Filter & Stopper

Ca. 1800s. Copper and brass with iron shaft to hold perforated center, controlled by thumbpress action; very large strap handle held by copper rivets. 8"H., 5¼"TD., $85.00.

This is not a common utensil. I once saw a similar utensil more primitively made in tin with a heavy wire trigger release, used for filling maple sugar molds.

Herb/Grinder/Spice Mill

Ca. 1890. Black cast iron; white cup interior and handle hold; for grinding pepper, cloves, and other small seed spices; can be screwed onto table or hung on the wall; ground contents fall into removable tin cup. 3¾"D; filler cup, 3¼"TD., $80.00.

Herb Grinder or Coffee Mill

Ca. late 1800s–1900. Tin hopper; cast iron fixtures; lift lid; mounted on a pine board for display; inside iron gears. $68.00.

Meal Grinder

For corn; dimmed red paint on cast iron with wood handle and emb: MODEL NO. 1 K, THE C.B. BELL CO., HILLSBORO, U.S.A. 14"H., $115.00.

Cornmeal Grater

Ca. 1700s. Homemade on a Georgia "holding"; jaggedly punched out tin on a pine board cut from a tree on the place; hard work grating ears of dried corn but while crude, this was effective in its service; a truly American kitchen helper. 30"L., 8½"W., $55.00.

Sleeve Grater

Blackened tin; wire; squared arc handle; slanted 1" on one side; half has coarsely punched holes, half is finely perforated. Dated Aug. 6, 1901. 7½"H., 2"TD., $30.00.

Food Slicers

Straight cutters, *ca. 1900s. Gray tin, wire frame. 11½"H., 4"W., $9.00. (Dealer's tag still in place.)*
Angled cutters, *ca. 1900s. Gray tin, wire frame; stamped "EVERSHARP VEGETABLE SLICER, N. Hampton St., Buffalo, N.Y. Pat applied for." 13"H., 4"W., $9.00.*

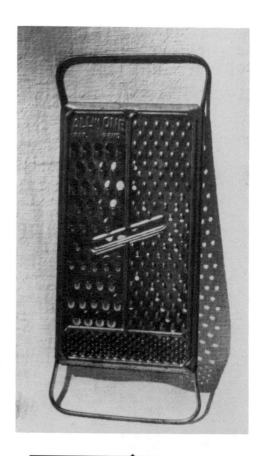

All-In-One Grater

Ca. 1940. Stamped ALL IN ONE, PAT. PEND. 10⅝"H., 4¼"W., $25.00.

Revolving Grater

Ca. 1930s. Tin, nickel, wood painted green; usually there were three grades of cutters – fine, medium, and coarse; grater drums could be removed. 8⅞"H., $25.00.

Graters

Half cylinder. *Ca. 1800s. Black japanned punched tin; one-piece wire frame; two base rest extensions; GILMORE PATENT. 9"H., 4½"W., $15.00.*

Half cylinder. *Ca. 1900s. Tin, wire, banded borders. 9"H., 4½"W., $8.00 – 9.50.*

Nutmeg Grater
Ca. late 1800s. Darkened tin with a plain straight back; perforated on a half-curved front; hinged lid lifts over a well for storing the aromatic peachstone-shaped nuts of the mace (the shell isn't wasted – separately grated and sold, or used in earlier kitchens – it has a stronger aroma and taste). $22.50.

Sifter/Shaker/Dredger
Ca. 1900s. Tin; old fashioned lap seaming; perforated lid, this one held grated nutmeg and/or other spices to drift over foods; large handle. (Also used as a muffineer for drifting sugar over muffins, etc.) 2½"H., 1½"Round., $18.00.

"Knuckle Duster" Grater

Ca. 1900s. Tin; punched holes for fine grating; arched strap-type handle. 8½"W., $18.00.

Grater

Ca. 1900s. Tin punched-out half round in solid frame; wire; pretty ring top. 4"H., 2⅞"W., $17.00.

Food Grater

Ca. 1700s–1800. Hand fashioned pine; side grooves on which a half-round tin framed grater with perforations in attempted swirl designs can be slid up and down, to release food bits and to clean the utensil; scalloped wood base; interesting, clever and rare. 6¼"W. curve; 13"H., 5½"W., $125.00 up to area.

One of those "sleepers" collectors hope to find at flea markets, etc.; this was purchased at a nominal price at an estate sale – and has now greatly increased in value.

Grater

Ca. early 1800s. Rare brass, hand fashioned; half round finely punched holes and twisted handle; one-piece frame. 6¼" curve, 13"H., $225.00.

Cream Whip

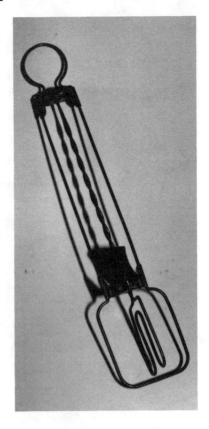

Ca. 1920. Black wire; tin plate controller is pushed down to the whipping blade, when the plate is released, the double blade turns and it whips the cream as the bar/plate is on its way back up to the ring top. Impr: HOR-LICK CREAM WHIP-PER. 9½"H., 2"W. beaters., $38.00.

Cream/Egg Whip

Galvanized tin; impr: FRIES; wood; wire; handle turns inside beaters; arched lid lift; at each base side one broad strip of tin is bent to form two side feet. 9½"H., $75.00.

Egg Beater/Cream Whip

Patent dates impr. for each year beginning Nov. 30, 1926 through Apr. 16, 1929. Stamped: LADD, United Royalties Corp., New York, U.S.A. No. 3W; rotary action turns blades; green wood handle grip and knob. The DOVER patent was issued ca. 1870 for rotary blades action, along with those of other makers. However, this popular form has been known for years as the DOVER, regardless of its manufactured origin. $38.00.

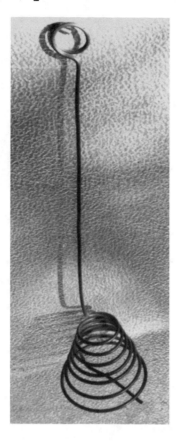

Cream Whip

Ca. 1890. Black tinned wire; one-piece spiraled with base rest; spring action in up and down pressure worked very well in whipping cream. 16"H., $35.00.

Whisk

All original; made from twigs first dried; wrapped ring to hold them together; suitable for whisking eggs and other very light foods. Early and rare. The dealer said she couldn't resist buying this. $25.00.

Ice Cream Server/Measure

Ca. late 1800s–1900. Pennsylvania origin; tin; turning the fancy wingnut on the bottom causes inside cup-length narrow both-sides-sharp blade to release the cold confection as the blade moves around the cup's edges. Uncommon. 7½"H., 4½"TD., $125.00.

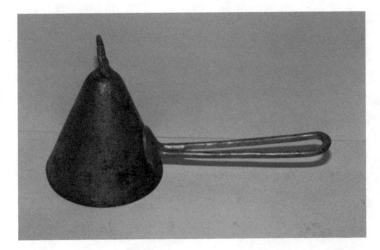

Ice Cream Scoop

Ca. 1900s. Cast iron; one of the early styles popular for shaping ice cream for cones and home desserts; tinned wire; thumb screw turns thin metal blade inside to release the cold treat as it moves around the sides of the scoop. 8⅜"L., $60.00.

Ice Cream Server

Ca. 1930s. Cast aluminum; thumb press device moves inside blade to release the ice cream. A brass fanciful Victorian handle was added when the original wooden one was broken off; somewhat elaborate for this type utensil but it worked and is fairly attrac-

tive. 9"L. This restoration is known as a "marriage" or "married-off," meaning that where one part of an object is damaged or missing, another related but not the original was added, most prevalent on furniture. In the beginning this "faking" was legitimate, and if not evident, buyers were usually told. Today, it benefits from tradition, and if not readily apparent, reliable dealers will point it out. (However, there are exceptions where one is so cleverly done it might even puzzle the dealer.) $48.00.

Ice Cream Disher

Ca. 1930s–40. Cast aluminum; natural finish wood; thumb press action on inside-bowl narrow sharp blade to remove ice cream from scoop. 8½"L., 2¼"W bowl, $22.50.

Ice Picks

Ca. early 1900s. Steel spear held inside a wood handle; thickly turned wood handle with original white paint now shabby. 6¼"H. Many of these were advertising giveaways. $9.00.

Ca. early 1900s. Squared handle, brass ferrule; steel spear held inside a wood handle. Printed in black: "Crystal Ice Delivery Co. Coal & Coke" on one side, two smudged North Tonawanda, N.Y. phone numbers on other. 6¾"L., $9.00.

Ice Picks

Ca. 1900s. Both original red painted handles, steel spears, metal ferrules; one squared and one rounded wood. 7"H. and 8"H., $9.00 each.

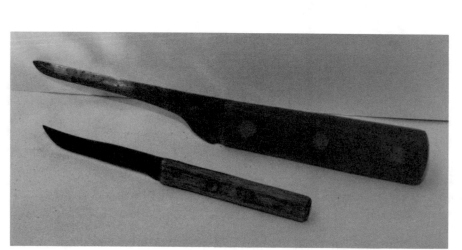

Knives

Ca. 1890–1910. Both steel and very sharp.
Butchering/boning, *walnut, copper rivets. $15.00.*
Paring, *hickory; Kentucky homemade. $10.00.*

Cleaver

Ca. 1890. For chopping meats into proper cookery parts as roasts, spareribs, able to crack the bones; heavy tool steel, wood, copper rivets, steel ferrule. 18½"L., 5½"W. blade, $35.00.

Utility/Paring Knife

Steel, wood; brass studs hold two handle parts together with knife metal between them. 11"L. Home handcarved wood knife case is 8¾"L., $12.50.

Knife Polisher
Ca. 1800s. Blue painted wood handle, brass collar; carborundum oval that could polish knives, etc. to a bright sheen. $10.00.

Kitchen Utility Knife
Ca. 1800s. Wood, nickeled steel blade, brass collar; nicked spot. $12.50.

Knife Sharpener
Ca. 1930s. Steel rollers which sharpened blades pulled between them; green painted wood handle; metal case; very durable and lasts for years. $25.00.

Knife Sharpener

Ca. 1900s. Cast iron, wood; gears are handle-turned, carborundum stones sharpen knife blade slipped between them. $28.00.

Lunch Pail

Ca. 1900s. Tin, wire. 4"H., 4½"TD., $25.00.

Dipper

Ca. 1800s. White, cobalt granite; flower-dots perforations unevenly spaced in bowl. 10½"L. handle; 3½"D.; 2"DP. dipper, $30.00.

Ladles

Ca. 1800s–1900s. All granite. The left one is pale blue and white and is uncommon, $35.00. The center one is gray and seen more often, $22.50. The right one is cobalt (also a dipper) and is the oldest, $39.50. The hanger is for display only.

Ladle and Skimmer

Both ca. 1700s. Both are blacksmith forged iron; note rat tail hangups; punched holes were not easy to make uniform and in precise lines; note the wrought work on the handles. Each 16½"L.; solid bowl, 4⅝"D., $55.00; punched bowl, 4¾"D., $55.00.

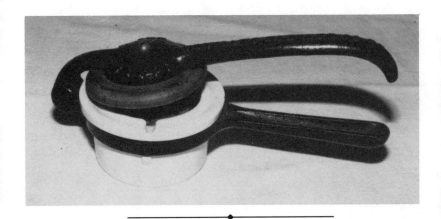

Lemon Squeezer

Ca. 1800's. Cast iron; wood; perforated porcelain to force juices through into a receptacle underneath. Emb: NEWMAN'S THE DRUM SQUEEZER, Pat. Aug 14, 1883. 2"H., 9"L., $75.00.

Lemon (Lime) Squeezer

Ca. 1800's. Hinged metal on wood; deep perforated cup in darker wood. ⅞" thick handles; 11¼"L., $75.00.

Lemon Squeezer

Ca. 1890s. Galvanized iron (to prevent rust): hinged two pieces, one pierced; fluted bowls. 8"L. $55.00.

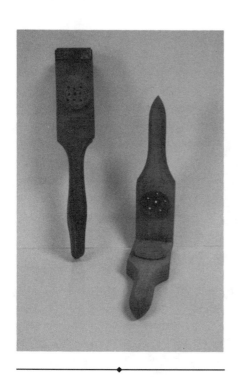

Lemon Squeezers

Ca. 1870s. Each has two pieces of hinged-joined hard maple; one has a perforated metal drip cup. $35.00.

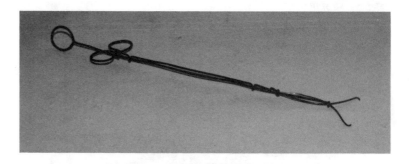

Utility Lifter

Ca. 1920s. Marked KLEVER KLAW, Kyser Bros., Lowell, Mich. Wire, twisted; pressure on the two thumb rings brings the claw ends together – for light things fallen behind something-with rags could clean out hard-to-reach places, might even pick up light vegetables out of a boiling pot. 14"L., $25.00.

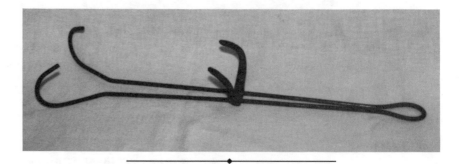

Plate Lifter

Ca. 1890s. Bent from one length of wire, this rare style has a cast iron adjustable slide. (User could wrap a heat-protective towel around the upper space in lieu of padded mitts.) 18"H., $65.00.

Potato Mashers or Vegetable Mashers

(Area known as Beetles). Used to mash or crush cooked foods. With this defined, after this first illustration, they will be referred to merely as **mashers.** *Ca. 1800s, each hand-carved from one-piece maple woods.*

Curvy handle turnings; mushroom finial. 10¾"H., $35.00.
Hefty inn/kitchen size; fat mushroom knob; handsome. 19¼"H., 4½"BD., $38.00.
Flat button knob handle; a chip gone; this may also have served as a herb masher. 9¾"H., $32.50.

Mashers

Ca. 1800s. While the weight is in the mashers, handles are usually longer – a lot or a little bit. Knobs give a better grip and keep the hand from slipping off while putting so much pressure down, possibly bruising the palm. Light maple. Each 9¾"H., 2¼"BD., $32.50 each.

Food Masher

Ca. very early 1800s. Hand turned hard maple; button top and center handle patterned with concentric rings. 15"H., $55.00.

Ca. early 1800s. Uncommonly styled handfashioned maple. 17½"H., $45.00.

Herb Masher
Ca. 1800s. Handcarved from one-piece maple; flat button top. 8"H., 2"D., $48.00.

Spatula/Cake Turner
Ca. late 1800s–1900. Galvanized tin; groove trimmed handle. 12½"H.; spade, 2⅞"W., $15.00.

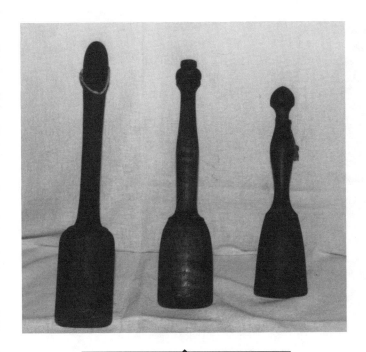

Mashers

Ca. 1800s–1900. All are maple; one-piece handcut. The largest one is very old; wire hangup through bored-through holes. 15½"H., 2¾"D., $35.00. The center one is rare tiger maple; fancy knob. 12½"H., 2¾"D., $65.00. The shortest one has pretty lathe turning; inverted acorn finial. 10"H., 2½"BD., $40.00.

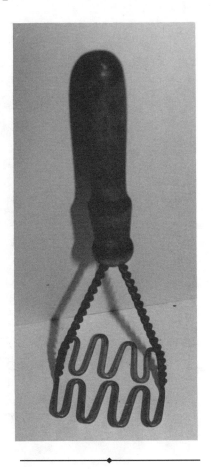

Masher

Ca. 1890. Twisted iron wire double tangs hold masher base to a wood handle on which original black paint is wear-dimmed. 9½"H., $23.50.

Mashers
Ca. 1800s–1900s. Far left: Cut from one piece of oak; the oldest shown in this photo; hangup holes through handle. 15"H., 2⅝"BD., $15.00. Second from left: Two pieces cut separately and joined. 13"H., $9.00. Next three: Each cut from one piece maple woods, one having a hangup rag strip; all are approximately 9¾", $12.50 each.

Herb Mashers/Crushers/Muddlers
Ca. 1800s. Second from right: handcut one-piece oak. 8"H., 2¾"BD., $25.00. Far right: Two pieces, joined maple. 5½"H., 3½"BD., $28.00.

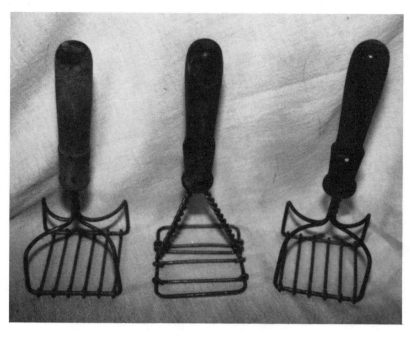

Mashers

Ca. 1800s–1900s. All are of heavy gauge wire and wood handles.
Left: Wide brass collar holding natural wood handle; only traces left of original black. 9¼"H. Center: Wishbone twists; better original paint. 9¼"H. Right: Utensil apparently seldom used, original paint. 9½"H., $25.00 – 32.50.

Spatula

Ca. 1840. Wrought iron. 12"H., $45.00.

Masher

Ca. 1880s. Bell-shaped curley maple, carved one piece. 11"H., 3¼"BD., $78.00.

Jar Lifter

Wood, wireware; spring action; gripping a jar at its ring top and lifting; wood bars are the hand supports in raising a hot jar of food from its steaming water cooking bath. 9½"H., $38.00.

Masher

Ca. 1890s. Wood; wireware. 8½"H., $9.00.

Meat Fret/Pounder

Rare in yellowware; turned hard maple handle extends through the crockery, slash-pinned at base in the early way to avoid shrinkage and loosening of the handle. This clear-glazed yellow earthenware has diamond-headed waffle bumps all way round. Emb: on base sides is "Pat. Dec. 25, 1877." Values on yellowware are escalating and the ware enjoys considerable buyers' interest. 10"H., 3"D., $85.00.

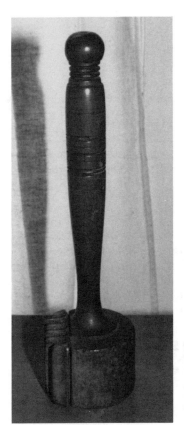

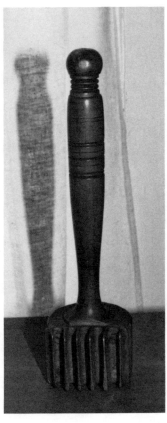

Meat Tenderizer/Pounder

Ca. 1800's. Rare type; three pieces in cast iron and walnut; handsomely turned handle with concentric rings and bulbous knob top on partial-round base; six connected frets make up a full round. 11"H., $95.00.

Meat Grinder

Ca, 1900's. Cast iron; green painted wood; turn bar fastens to table; for grinding meat cut into small chunks or any other food suitable for this size appliance; emb: REGAL. 8⅞"H., 2½"TD., $35.00.

Nutcracker

Ca. 1800's. Gilded cast iron; two parts screwed together; raising the handle-tail opens the corrugated inside jaws where a nut in its shell can be placed; lowering the handle firmly closes the mouth with enough pressure to crack the nut's shell. 4⅝"H., 11½" top to end of tail, $75.00.

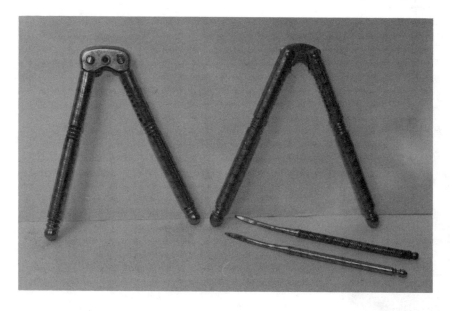

Nutcrackers

Ca. 1899-1900's. Each nickeled iron; two hinged corrugated sides holding a nut brought together crack the shell. 4⅞"H.

Picks

Nickeled iron; decorated handles with spear points used to remove the kernels; typically six picks in a set. Some sort of nutcracking device has been made for centuries – many of wood and steel. 4¾"H.

$25.00 for the set.

Nutmeg Grater

Ca. late 1800s–1900s. Tiny wooden gears inside activated by turning the large side screw; French origin. $58.00.

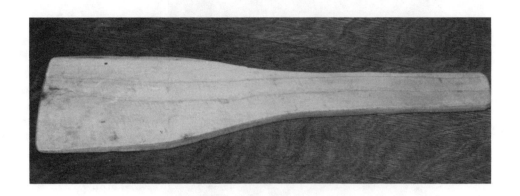

Peel/Utility Board

Ca. 1800s. Hickory; handcut. 15½"H., $18.00.

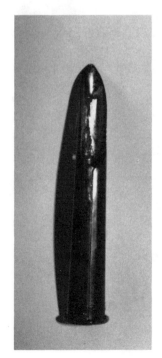

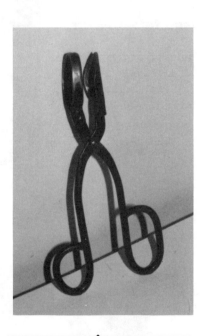

Pineapple Corer and Peeler

Ca. 1930s. Heavy tinned metal; the sharp pointed end cores out the fruit's eyes and the side blade slices off the spiny harsh skin. 5"H., $28.00.

Pineapple Eye Remover/Snip/Huller

Ca. 1880. Iron and iron wire black japanned; scissors style; very sharp-sided spoon digs under and lifts an eye and the other open round comes down to snip it off; quicker and much safer than using a pointed knife to dig out the imbedded eyes. 6"H., $35.00.

Bread Maker/Mixer/Kneader

Tin; cast iron fixtures; strips underneath to fasten the appliance to a table or bench, the screw-hold missing; (here set on a pail for display only); the wood knobbed handle cranks the inside paddle; emb: UNIVERSAL, LANDERS, FRARY & CLARK, NEW BRITAIN, CONN. U.S.A.; Pat. dates Dec. 11, 1900 through Dec. 25, 1906. 12"H., 13¾"TD., $58.00+.

Dough Bowl/Raiser/Mixer

Ca. 1880. Handcarved from one piece of pine; with long usage it is in fine condition – many chopping marks. 17¾"L., 9"W., 3"DP., $175.00.

Flour Advertising Mirror

Black printed on white, shows factory buildings. Front reads, "SHAWNEE MILLING CO., Good Millers For Over 30 Years;

SHAWNEE'S BEST and CLIMAX FLOUR, Poultry and Molasses FEEDS, SHAWNEE, OKLAHOMA." Reverse side is an unblemished mirror; often carried in pockets, bags, or hung by the kitchen door. 2⅜"D., $35.00.

Dredger

Ca. 1870s. Japanned tin; wire, small holes in convex removable top; to scatter flour, spices, salt, or pepper on meat during roasting; its 4½" extra-long handle could reach out over pots, or foods being turned on a spit. Cup 4"H., 3½"D., $45.00.

Dough Bowl/Raiser

Ca. 1840–50. Handcarved pine; could've been for a large family but probably for inn-size kitchens; all one piece, wide shelf-like extensions each end and the wood grains match; has been well used but resisted damage. 8"H., 39"L., 16"W., $265.00+.

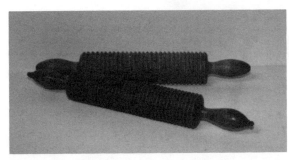

Cookie Rollers

Ca. 1860. Maple; each 12"L., $39.00 each.

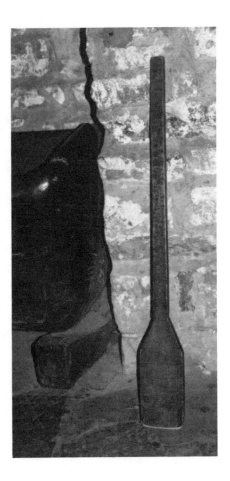

Dough Mixer/Raiser

Seen in the "Castle" kitchen at Old Fort Niagara, N.Y. 3" thick wood, 29"H., 30"W. The **mixing paddle** *is handcut oak. It took a lot of strength to handle. N.P.A.*

Rolling Pin

Opaque milk glass, lathe-turned wood; ends emb: IMPERIAL MFG. CO., CAMBRIDGE, OHIO, U.S.A.; JULY 26, 1921. 19"L., $95.00.

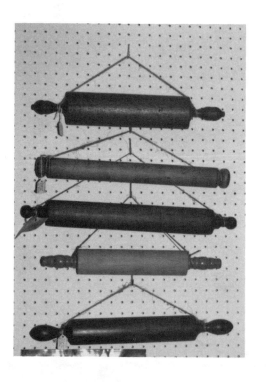

Rolling Pins

Ca. late 1800s–early 1900s. All one-piece handcarved pine or maple, $55.00, except for the one second from the bottom which was factory made, $10.00.

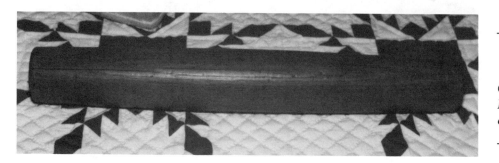

Rolling Pin

Ca. 1800s. Carved from one-piece oak. 17½"L., $68.00.

Rolling Pin

Ca. early 1800s. Hand-turned Rock Maple; heavy. 17½"L, 2" end D., $58.00.

Rolling Pin

Ca. 1800s. Carved from one piece of maple; acorn finial handle ends. 17"L., $78.00.

Flour Sifter
Ca. 1900s. Tin, wire; emb: Patented, Made in U.S.A.; green wood knob. 3½"H., 3"D., $18.00.

Muffin Pan
Ca. 1900. Tin; six individual cups. 6"L., 4"W., $10.00.

Pasta/Noodle Roller

*Wooden and cast iron MODEL, inventor JOHN TABER, WASHINGTON, D.C.; the torn bits of paper are the original tag which was on the roller upon submission at the U.S. Govt. Patent Office. **Rare** kitchen device collectible. (It is said that Marco Polo brought the process of making noodles back to Italy from China.) $195.00.*

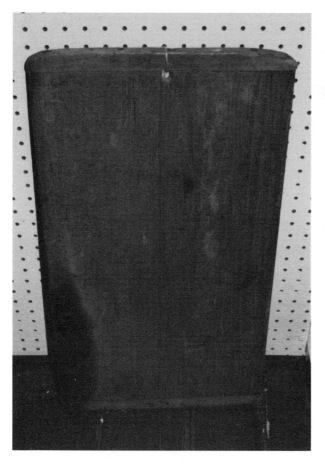

Dough Board

Ca. late 1800s. Handcut pine; thick breadboard ends were to prevent warping; might have been made as an individual unit for rolling all sorts of doughs, but more commonly they were just pulled out of a cabinet – as is a drawer – or fit down inside a dough raiser, to be laid on the lid in preparing pastries. (The oil stain may be from a kerosene lamp spill when the cook was working after dark, kneading bread doughs or rolling the next day's pie crusts.) $38.00.

Dough Board Scraper

Ca. 1700s. Smithy iron forged; spade is somewhat longer than usually seen; many found today were made in Pennsylvania German communities. $55.00.

Lard Can

Ca. 1900s. Tin; tightly lidded. 5"H., 5"TD., 4½"BD., $10.00.

Flour Sifter

Ca. 1910. Tin; green painted wood handle; wire. 7"H., 4¾"D., $18.00.

Flour Sifters

Ca. 1925. Mechanical action forced dry ingredients through the mesh. The smaller one is tin, wood; longer wire turner with green knob; marked MADE IN U.S.A. and Pat No. 17582975. 3½"H., 3"TD., $15.00. The larger one is tin; emb. markings from two cups to five cups on calibrated sides; also: BROMWELL'S MEASURING SIFTER, GUARANTEED; original green paint on handle and knob. $20.00.

Sifter (Flour/Sugar)

Ca. 1864. All original; cedar; wood pegged; each 8½"W end extends into bracket feet; four inside crosswise dowels plus turn-shaped handle; pushed back and forth by the handle, (flour) sifts through the finely meshed cloth screening; it all comes apart for cleaning. **Rare.** *$275.00+. Box only 9"H., 10"W.*

Flour Sifter

Ca. 1890s–1900. Couldn't resist adding this one; a dealer found it lying beside discarded "things" when a neighbor near her mall moved away. Tin, yellow wood knob; cast iron and wire; handle plus inside parts pushed ingredients back and forth across the mesh, forcing them through the flat bottom screen; intact and workable after a good cleaning; the fun of discovering it is reflected in the price. 7½"H., 4"TD., $9.00.

Potato Peeler

Ca. 1920. More properly – a scraper, tin with scalloped edges; for scraping off thin-skinned potatoes; arc handle; the under (worker) side is coal-like black shining hamlinite, a mixture of coarse grit. $65.00.

Skimmer

Ca. 1870. Smithy wrought iron; convenient out-curved handle and deep bowl. 6"H. bowl, 4½"W., $35.00.

Slaw Cutter

Ca. 1880–1910. Uncommon style; wood and tin; two pieces; lower section is corrugated; wire slides at the sides. 13½"H., 5"W., $45.00.

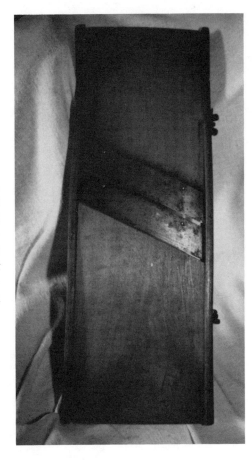

Food Slicer/Vegetable Cutter

Ca. 1870. Also kown as **shredder, cabbage,** *or* **slaw cutter/kraut board.** *Iron blades angled 30°, could be regulated by wing-screws for desired cutting sizes; galleried pine board. Originating in France and first called "chou-crou," kraut, the salt-pickled delicacy was soon adopted in Germany. 17½"H., 6¼"W., $25.00.*

Shredder/Slaw Cutter

Sharp coarse graters; emb: THE WONDER GRATER, Reg. U.S. Pat. Off.; rolled top to fit over a bowl, etc.; also has the patent numbers. Dated 1930s. 8½"H., 4½"W., $25.00.

Vegetable Cutters/Slicers

The cutter on the left has a differently styled cutter and a natural finished maple handle. Ca. Early 1900s. 9"L. The other two have fluted metal blades; wire; original green and worn white painted handles; brass ferrule; for garnishing slices of raw vegetables. Ca. late 1800s–1900. Each 7"L., $20.00 – 22.50.

Food Ricer/Press

Ca. 1925–30. Hinged cast iron handles in up and down action, with plate down in the perforated cup; held by an iron shaft forced cooked vegetables and potatoes through zinc-plated tin for rice-size bits; a change from serving them mashed. 3"H., 10¾"L., $18.00.

Strainer

Ca. 1900s. Tin; hollow handle with closed end; fine meshed wire screen in high collar; soldering; slanted sides. $25.00.

Egg Whip/Whisk/Beater

Tinned wire; twisted handle. (Might have also been used for cream.) 8"L., $28.00.

Strainer

Ca. 1900s. Wire; fine mesh; brass ferrule holds wood handle with traces of original green paint; ears fit over a bowl's rim. 8½"H., 3½"D., $20.00.

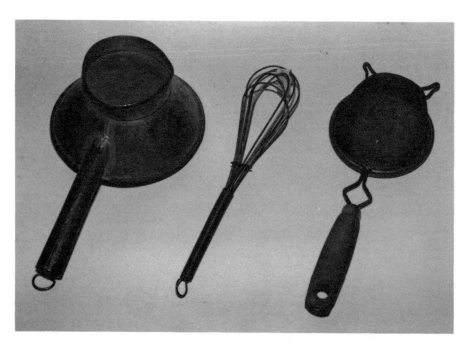

Strainer

Ca. 1920s–30s. Wire, fine wire mesh; footed metal frame; tin collar; side fancy ears to fit over a bowl; can rest on a table. 4"H., 7¼"TD., $22.00.

Strainer

Ca. 1920s–30s. Wire, fine wire mesh; metal frame, tin collar; worn original red paint on a wood handle; base ring surrounds a flattened bottom; small ear hooks to fit over a drip container. 8½"TD., $25.00.

Strainers

The larger one is ca. 1920s–30s. Curved wire holding base of meshed bowl. 8½"TD., $23.00. The smaller one has most of the original red paint worn off of the handle. 5"TD., $20.00.

Strainer

Ca. 1860. Milk cooling pan handy when another strainer was needed; slant sides tin with joints lapped and rolled (some later soldered) in early way of seaming; crudely tin-snipped a center-base hole in the pan and inserted a wire mesh round soldered in; many wear signs but no worn-through damage. 5¾"H., 12"TD., $35.00.

Sieve

Ca. 1890's. Tin, wire; slanted slides to a perforated bottom through which hand-shaking sideways sifts flour or other dry ingredients; wet and/or juicy foods drip through. $28.00.

Funnel

Ca. 1800's. Galvanized tin; narrow throat for filling bottles (with medicines or home-canned juices, etc.) or any small containers having limited openings. $38.00.

Sieve

Ca. 1800's. Bentwood wrapped, nailed, and long-wire stapled frame surrounds the horsehair strainer; used by shaking back and forth to sift contents; unlike many sifters, there are no moving parts; only the hands supply the action. 4½"H., 8¾"D., $45.00.

Spoon

Ca. early 1800s. Handcarved in bleached wood; aside from carved hanging hook it has an underside small ledge (each part of the one piece) so the spoon will lie flat on a table without tipping or spilling. 15"L., $45.00.

Dipper/Spoon

Ca. 1800s. Handcarved maple; curved handle with extended hook. 11½"L., $125.00.

Spoon

Ca. 1900s. For mixing, stirring, wherever needed; wood with some end wear-offs; could also "reach in" for tasting! $9.00.

Spoons

Ca. 1800s. All handcarved maple. 11½"L., 8½"L., 7½"L., $9.50 – 12.50.

Wooden Bowl

Ca. 1840–50. Rare tiger maple; wide rim band to better hold it; these were much used with choppers/mincing knives; hence the inside-bottom shallow cuts. (That chore was customarily holding the bowl on an apron-clad lap with one hand, wielding a chopper with the other); satin patina. 17¾"L., 9"TD., 3"BD., $225.00+.

Stirring Spoons

The shorter spoon is thinly carved one-piece maple. Ca. 1900s. 10"L., $4.50 – 6.00. The longer spoon is carved, two-piece maple so that if the handle became worn or broken off another of the same dimensions could be fit into the bowl's collar. Ca. 1850–60. 14"L., $22.50.

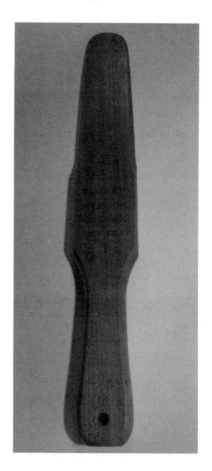

Advertising Lifter/Spatula

Ca. 1900s. Maple, for lifting slices of pies, etc.; both sides printed in black: Wrigley's Spearmint, Doublemint, Juicy Fruit. 13½"H., 1¼" to 1⅞"W., $25.00.

Toaster

Ca. 1920s. Pyramid; blackened tin and wire; non-electric, was set on stove and heat came up the inside; four slices of bread were toasted at one time and then turned over after one side had browned; pedestal-type holders against which bread slices were leaned. 5"H., 6½" square base, $19.00.

Yellowware Bowl

Ca. late 1800s. Rarely seen with blue birds and white clouds framed in a paler yellow; tiny no-harm nick. 3¼"H., 7⅛"TD., $78.00.

Yellowware Mixing Bowls

Ca. late 1800s. Clear-glazed earthenware, its clay establishing the natural yellow color; seldom marked; the smaller sizes more uncommon. First American handmade and then machine-produced, largely by Ohio potters (East Liverpool best known); it also came from Pennsylvania and Vermont but in limited production; intended as utility ware for everyday usage in homes and dairies. Larger size, 4½"H., 8¼"TD., 4¼"BD., $45.00. Smaller size, 3¼"H., 6¾"TD., 3¼"BD., $50.00.

The Expansion of Utensils

To mention "utensils" almost automatically brings to mind the idea of smaller "instruments" (or tools), extending the range of our hands' capabilities. With such boundaries restrictive and often confusing, that word also properly includes "vessels," covering a multitude of material things in kitchens from primitive to present. And so we have ... **Kitchenwares.**

Mortar and Pestle

*Ca. 1700s. The **mortar** is handcarved chestnut; no harm to value on such an artifact is the wire added at a later time when steady wear and age had taken their toll. 6"H., 5"TD. The **pestle** is a natural stone, probably after diligent searching found in this oblong shape, worn even more round on the edges from being used; foods, herbs, and juices stained _ and who knows what else the housewife may have pounded into paste or pulverized herein. 7"L., 3"W., 2½ – 3 lbs. wt., $275.00+.*

With a mortar the bowl and the pestle a pounding rod, these helpers have been used in kitchen cookery from the 15th century; converting many substances, they were made of wood, metal, ceramics, and stone in many sizes, some plain, others decoratively cast in iron. Roasted coffee was first mortar pounded (constituting grinding).

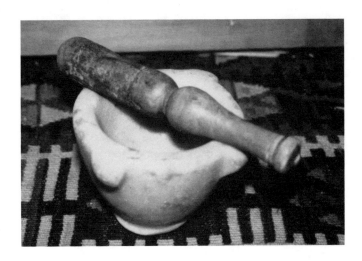

Mortar and Pestle

Ca. early 1800s. The thick stoneware mortar is crookedly attractive with four pulled-out "ears," on two of which rests the heavy gracefully-turned wood pestle, dented and scored from over 150 years of turning raw ingredients into pastes and powders. $175.00.

Mortar and Pestle

Ca. 1800s. Stoneware and wood; mortar has a pouring lip; pestles tip is button-flat; 5½" length fits into the ironstone terminal; pounded and crushed spices, salt and sugar chunks and more; while stoneware is available, there are fewer in this smaller size. 2½"H., 4"D., $85.00.

Mortar and Pestle

Ca. 1870. Mortar is smoothly cast and polished iron. 5½"H., 5⅞"D rim. Pestle has flared end. 8⅜"L. The two pieces weigh about 12 lbs., $125.00+.

Mortar and Pestle

Ca. 1870. Inverted bell-shaped iron mortar. 6¾"H. Pestle has top knob and is pitted. 9"L. Overall weight about 10–12 lbs. Apothecaries used many cast iron sets. $125.00+.

Herb Drying Board

Ca. 1900. Original red paint now faded; old square-head nails. 9½"H., 14"L., $75.00.

Herb Mixing Bowl

Carved two pieces; turned handle set into side; used in both home kitchens and apothecary shops for mixing powders and home remedy medicinal recipes. 4"L. handle, 3½"TD., $48.00+.

Lunch Pails in Carrier

Ca. 1890. Scarce collectible, few were made as they were quite perishable, particularly under their usage handling; pale apple green is the primary granite color with liquid enameling applied for bright apple blosssoms and hovering bees; the iron strap lengths slip out and down to release the pails; then when they are again set on top of each other, the bands secure them to be lifted and carried by the wood handle. Set on the stove, they were heated before taken to school, work, fields, or other places. The dealer felt there is really no precise way to accurately evaluate them and so normal circumstances of her own costs were the criteria for pricing. $195.00 – 225.00.

Granite Cups

Ca. 1890. Rarities. Pale blue and cobalt granite; mustard ring below rims; strikingly colorful flowers, more so than on the lunch pails. 3¼"H., 3"TD.

In trying to imitate the look of natural granite, American makers achieved to a large degree its appearance but lacked its hard durability. However, featured at Philadelphia's 1876 Exposition, it was highly advertised and well received. It represents the "look of country" many folks want in their kitchens today, prices escalating accordingly. $55.00 each.

Lunch Box

All original; hard used; japanned red and black tin; hinged lid; label: MOORE'S PATENTED LUNCHBOX; kitchen-packed to be carried to school, work shifts, fields, etc. 2½"H., 7"W., 4"DP., $18.50.

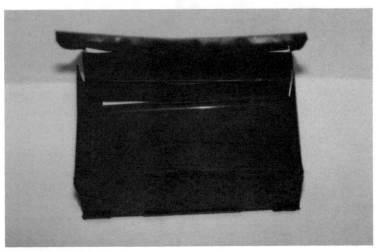

Lunch Pail

Speckled white on cobalt granite; wire bail and handle grip; three units all fit into the pail, the cup upside down over the open center. 12"H. to handle top; 10"L., 6½"W., $122.50.

Chocolate molds were generally made of easily malleable and inexpensive tinplate with attention to detailing. Especially popular in the early 1900s, many Pennsylvania housewives, needing extra income, purchased the molds from commerical makers of the sweet products to prepare the novelties for sale from their own kitchens. Few were successful. Today they are sought for kitchen decorating – or wherever else in the home one's fancy dictates.

Chocolate Mold

"Skippy Skimmer." Ca. 1920s–30s. He represents a newspaper comic strip character. Long clips hold the sides together. Boy-like, his hands are in his pockets and on his face is an engaging expression; his clothes are typical of that northern European region. 6½"H., 4"W., $98.00 up to area.

Chocolate Mold

Ca. 1800s–1900s. Running rabbit; ears laid back; good eye expression; two separate with three joiners. 4½"H., 8½"L. Animals remain popular in chocolate fancies. $115.00.

Chocolate Bars Mold

Ca. 1890–1900s. Japanned tin; made 24 bars at a time; when the confection had hardened, strips could be lifted out. 11"L., 6¾"W., $55.00.

Chocolate Molds

Four rabbits with backpacks. White metal and tin plate. Closed, 4"H., 7"L., $135.00.

Chocolate Mold

Easter eggs. Ca. 1920–30s. From an Ohio collection. Each side 9½"L., 5½"W., $118.00.

Chocolate Mold

Easter egg. Ca. 1920s. In these chocolate eggs, the crisscross sections were planned for adding decorations to the top of the formed and hardened candy – most often in several colored icing patterns. Two separate parts clip-held together; such eggs were molded in countless sizes both smaller and larger. 4½"H., 7"L., $78.00.

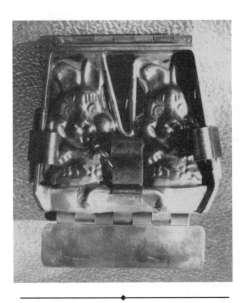

Chocolate Mold

Twin rabbits. Ca. 1900s. Fat-cheek bunnies once molded and hardened, would be individually ejected from their heavy three-clip bottom and top smaller hinged mold. 5½"H., 4½"W., $110.00.

Chocolate Mold

Rabbit. Ca. 1920s. Heavy gauge tin; hinged two parts; original clips missing. (Black enamel rubbed off something else set against the mold.) $48.00.

The following are clear glazed stoneware molds with patterns deeply impressed into each inside base, intended for cold jellied desserts, blancmange (made from gelatin or starch substances with milk), and similar dishes. When firm, the solids are taken out, placed upside down on serving platters, thus revealing the attractive designs. (These particular molds were gathered together over a period of years. A New Hampshire collector, having purchased as a home a former stagecoach inn, kept them there, occasionally displaying them to his friends.)

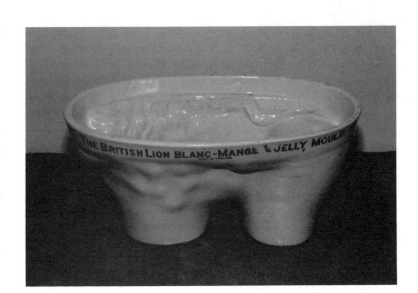

Double Lion Mold

Printed: THE BRITISH BLANC-MANGE & JELLY MOULD. 5½"H., 10⅝"L., $385.00.

Pig Mold

6"H., 7"L., $350.00.

Lion Mold

6⅞"H., 5"L., $295.00.

Person Milking Cow Mold

5¾"H., 8"L., $525.00.

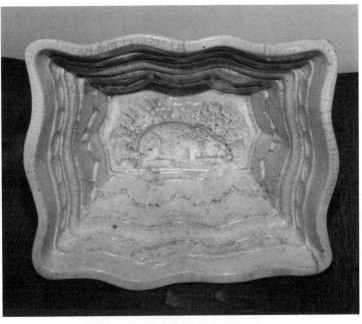

Crouched Rabbit

5"H., 6½"L., $250.00.

Partridge Mold

Very old and rare. 7½"H., 8½"L., $550.00.

Angel Mold

Ornate. 5⅝"H., 7⁷⁄₁₆"L., $425.00.

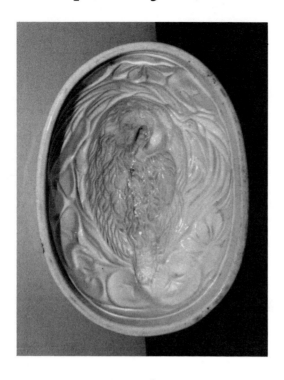

Eagle Mold

*Ornate, marked: J & G MEAKIN. 5¼"H., 7"L.,
$600.00.*

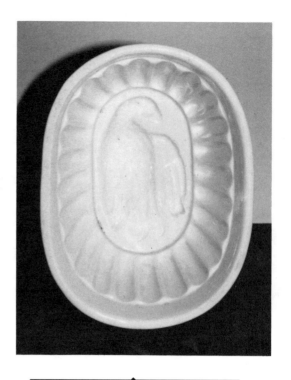

Eagle Mold

*Head in turned position. 6"H., 8"L.,
$425.00.*

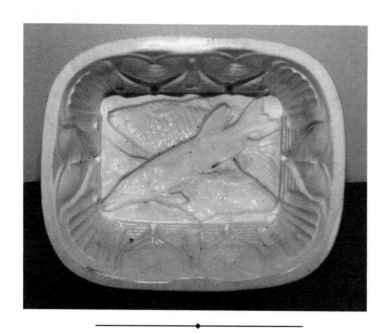

Three Fish Mold

Heart border, rare. 5¾"H., 7½"L., $575.00.

Fish Mold

Rare. 6½"H., 8⅛"L., $445.00.

Fancy Design Mold

Intricate design of flowers, leaf stems, curlicues, and a medallion resembling a coat of arms; convex-concave side pattern. 2¼"H., 8"L., $295.00.

Ear of Corn Mold

Rim curves, realistic grains. 2½"H., 8"L., $250.00.

Sheaf of Wheat Mold

Diamond points; center-tied sheaves; deep wall flutings, each particle distinct. 2¾"H., 7¾"L., $395.00.

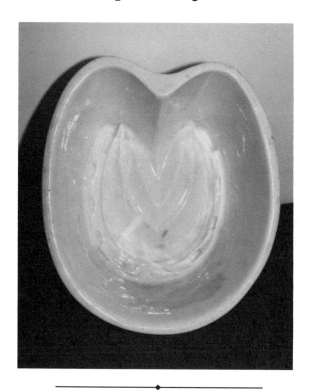

Horseshoe Mold

Rare. 6¾"H., 7⅝"L., $395.00.

Three-Legged Grape Cluster Mold

This illustrates the bottom of a three-legged mold. 8¼"H., 5¼"L., $300.00.

Unusual Pineapple Pattern Mold

This shape is uncommon. 3¾"H., 6⅜"L., $315.00.

Geometric Pattern Mold

5½"H., 8"L., $225.00.

Pea Pod Mold

4$\frac{1}{16}$"H., 5$\frac{3}{8}$"L., $250.00.

Large Pea Pod Mold

6"H., 8$\frac{15}{16}$"L., $295.00.

Shell Mold

5$\frac{1}{2}$"H., 7"L., $250.00.

Large Floral Mold

8"H., 10"L., $325.00.

Basket of Strawberries Mold

Rare. 4⁵⁄₁₆"H., 5¹¹⁄₁₆"L., $335.00.

Fruit Cluster Mold

Pineapple, grapes, strawberries and more.
Small nick and crack. 5⅝"H., 7"L., $250.00.

Birds Mold

Six birds in all. 5½"H., 7³⁄₁₆"L., $410.00.

Pears Mold

5¾"H., 8⅛"L., $195.00.

Hummingbird and Fruit Mold

6¾"H., 8½"L., $475.00.

Floral Mold

Rose, daisy, and thistle. Signed COPELAND.
6³⁄₁₆"H., 7¹³⁄₁₆"L., $325.00.

Grape Cluster Mold
Large. 7¾"H., 9¼"L., $275.00.

Grape Cluster Mold
Ornate. 7¼"L., $285.00.

The following are miniature molds.

Grape Cluster on Leaf Mold
Three legs, one missing. 2¾"H., 3¾"L., $165.00.

Floral Mold
5¹⁄₁₆"H., 7"L., $135.00.

Sheaf of Wheat Mold
Signed "John Alcock." 3½"H., 4½"L., $265.00.

Corn Mold
2½"H., 4¼"L., $175.00.

Grape Cluster
2¼"H., 3¾"L., $250.00.

Squirrel Mold
Rare, slight damage at rim. 3¼"H., 4"L., $375.00.

Molds

Ca. 1800s. Rare, beautiful in tinned copper, expertly detailed; for jellied dishes for the table as sweets or piquant savories (a word often seen in mention of old cookery).

Ear of corn on the stalk. *The sides are elaborately decorated in a heavy manner with double ridges at the corn and around the scalloped base; note how each grain on the ear stands out clearly.* **Resting lion.** *Note the expression in the eyes; even the fluted sides have a line pattern, diamonds at the top making them appear as draperies. Each 6"H., 5"W. Corn, $425.00. Lion, $475.00.*

Cheese Mold/Strainer

Ca. 1800s. Black heart-shaped tin with pierced dots and dashes for a design on the molded food; three short legs; Pennsylvania Dutch (German settlers) origin. 3"H., 4½"TD., $170.00.

Ice Cream Mold

Ca. 1900s. Christmas bells; tin, hinged and held by clips; five individual servings on a frame with a solid top. $95.00.

As an inexpensive and easily workable metal, tinplate was popularly used by tinners in the American colonies as early as the 1700s, creating all sorts of fanciful dishes of jellies, ice cream, puddings, and the like.

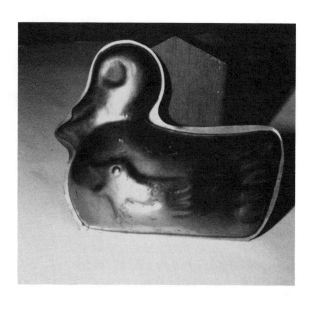

Chicken Cake Mold

Separately cast iron in two pieces to be joined; holes where the chicken was held together by a fastener; (dealer was holding it together with cord); handle-holds each side at the neck. 7"H., 8½"L., 3¾"W. at base, $68.00.

Half Bird Chocolate Mold

Tin; rusty on the back but could make a cabinet piece with that side not showing; different in that the wing is a baby bird with its mouth wide open; was originally hinged on the bottom. 4¼"H., 5"L., $68.00.

Springerle Print Board

Ca. 1850. A specialty of the Pennsylvania Dutch, these rather hard delicately anise-flavored cookies are more often seen during the holidays, known regionally as Christmas cookies. Handcarved in the keystone state from native pine, this board pressed into the soft dough has the customary assortment of designs along with deep grooves which enable the springerles, once they are baked to be individually separated. Each cookie emerges from the oven with its own surface picture. Here four completed figures are colonial ladies, one wearing a fichu (ornamental three-cornered neckerchief), another carrying a basket on her arm, a townsman in a high hat, and a uniformed soldier, along with a tree and flowers. Two additional carvings were started on the two bottom panels but never finished. At the top of the split-off sides are other indefinable beginnings. The partial aspects considerably increase the value since others are completed. 6½"L., 3½"W., $295.00.

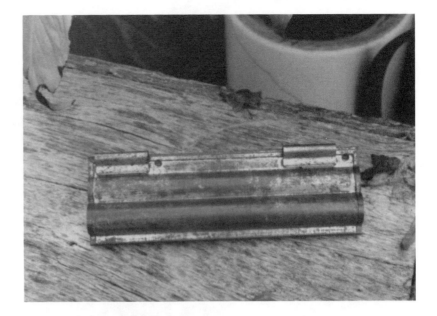

Cookie Mold

Ca. 1800s. Clips held the one-piece, roll-shaped galvanized tin; a length of dough was solidly packed in; after baking, it could be removed in one piece and cut into whatever cookie thicknesses were desired; this in a playing-card club design; the whole procedure was much faster than cutting individual cookies for baking. $78.00.

Dough Print

Ca. 1860. Handcarved one-piece maple; scalloped framing of flowers, leaves, and seed pods. $225.00.

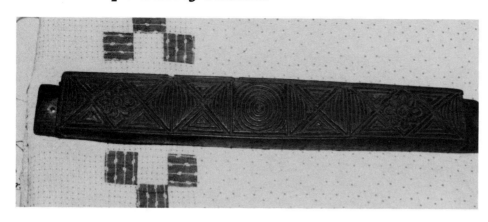

Dough Print

Ca. 1850–60. Handcarved wood in circle, diamonds, lines, and flower patterns; back extends about 2" at each end for handholds to press the designs into the dough; grooved for dividing into individual pastries. $155.00.

Redware Mold

Turban/Turk's Head. Red earthenware glazed; swirled sides and closed center horn; underglaze brown sponged. 4"H., 9¼"TD., $150.00.

Turk's Head Mold

Ca. 1800s. Finely cast iron, swirls; diamond points; wide horn; sometimes called baking dishes, these are actually molds in metal or pottery, making cakes swirled like turbans. 3¼"H., 9"TD., $95.00.

Rice/Vegetable Mold

Ca. 1870s–1890s. Polished tin; center tube makes for even steaming or baking; tightly clamped lid at each side has a wire ring lift. When contents were "done" they were removed and placed upside down on a platter or fancy dish so the bottom design of the tin would appear at the top of the food mold. Could also be used without the lid as a mold for jellied dishes and a Charlotte Russe – a Russian dessert of cake with a custard-gelatin or whipped cream filling-first being sure the tin was lightly moistened, this true too for the food molds with a little oil or grease. $58.00.

Cooking Pot

White flecked cobalt granite; wire bail; tilt bar circle; lid with an arc bar. $48.00.

Maple Sugar Mold

Ca. 1830–40. Pine (considered the best wood to release hardened sugar cakes more easily); deeply handcarved heart, spade, and diamond on a thick slab; New England origin. 16"L., 4"W., 2"DP., $265.00.

Maple Sugar Molds

Ca. 1800s. Handcarved five maple slabs, each one having an extended handle; various designs as animals, birds, a fish, diamonds, and a shell among them. $128.00 each.

Melon/Pudding Mold

Ca. late 1800s. Tin made in base and lid with an iron rod through the center (got the heat into the middle of the pudding for more even cooking); ring handle top and bottom. 9"L., 6¼"W. base, $50.00.

Melon/Pudding Mold

Ca. 1890s. Tin; two pieces, wire; ribbed top resembles half a cantaloupe (muskmelon); for steaming or baking; on base: "Liquid 2 Qts." – other words not readable. 6"H., 4⅛"W., $55.00.

Melon/Pudding Mold

Ca. late 1800s. Tin made in two parts as base and lid; wire; melon-ribbed top. 7¼"L., 5½"W., $55.00.

Food Mold

White granite on fluted metal; minor chips; almost no rim wear. 3"H., 5¾"D., $45.00.

Pudding Mold

Ca. 1890s. Deep tin boiler/ steamer; inside full height tube for even baking "doneness"; lid with wire handle has tightly tin clamped sides; made in the old way of seam wrapping-joinings., $55.00.

Turban (Turk's Head) Mold

Tiny white swirls on gray granite; long large horn; unusual; very old and fortunately has few scars; rim is cobalt. 5⅞"H., 9¾"D., $195.00.

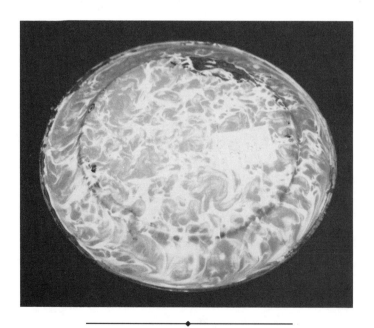 

Mold

Ca. 1890. Tin; deeply scalloped sides; cup size tube. 8½"D., $35.00.

Pie Pan

Ca. 1800s. Photo shows bottom of pan; uncommon pale blue and white granite; some wear. 3"H., 9"D., $65.00.

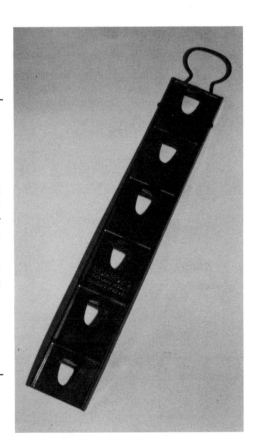

Pie Rack

Ca. 1872. Rare; ornately cast iron for wall hanging; five heavy gauge iron wire frames (shelves) held five pie pans for storing when not in use – but just as often for cooling pans of baked pastries. Dated Oct. 20, 1872. 18½"H., 3¼"W., $168.00.

Granite Pie Pans on Shelves

Top two are swirled cobalt and white; the bottom one is all-over cobalt. Top pan, 8½"D; lower two, 9"D., $45.00.

Potato Baker Rack

Tin; wire; potatoes stuck on sharp flaps are oven-baked six at a time; emb: RUMFORD, THE WHOLESOME BAKING POWDER, Pat'd. Aug. 17, 1909. 13¾"H., 2¼"W., $95.00.

Pie Rack

Ca. early 1900s. Tin wash on iron wire; can sit flat on a counter; three shelves plus bottom rest. 11"H., 7"D. rounds., $125.00.

Pie Pan

Ca. 1920s. Gray granite. 8"D., $30.00.

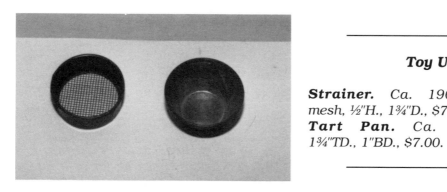

Toy Utensils

Strainer. _Ca. 1900s. Tin and wire mesh, ½"H., 1¾"D., $7.00._
Tart Pan. _Ca. 1900s. Tin. ⅞"H., 1¾"TD., 1"BD., $7.00._

Child's Kitchenware

Cookie Box. _Old tin, faded original red paint; hinged lid full 4" width. 4"H., 6"L., $15.00._
Muffin Tins/Flat Tea Cakes. _Old tin, six individual spaces on a frame 4"H., 6"L. Four individual spaces on a frame 4" square., $15.00._
Tin Cup. _Old tin, gray (also a measuring cup); stamped: C.A. CHAPMAN, GENEVA, N.Y. 3¾"H., 3"TD., 2½"BD., $22.50._

Tin Kitchenware

Eating-table Spoons. _Ca. 1900s. Stamped; grooved handles. 5¼"L., $5.00._
Cookie/Cake Cutters. _Ca. 1879's–80s. Diamond, 1"W. arc strap handle; star, spot-soldered handle., $38.00._
Cake Pans. _Ca. 1900s. Mini pie and individual tart pans. Larger one, 5"TD.; smaller two, 4"TD., $9.00 – 12.50._

Patty (Pattie) Pans

Ca. 1870s. Scalloped sides tin bakers; their pastries made as many as possible at a time due to the tedium of cutting and shaping of the dough. Larger one, 4"TD.; smaller one, 3"TD., $15.00 – 18.00.

Muffin/Corn Cake Pan

Ca. 1885–90s. Could bake more than one at a time; four tins on an iron frame having a decoratively twisted handle; decorating comes in unexpected places, don't you think? Each tin 4"D., $55.00+.

Muffins/Flat Tea Cakes

Ca. 1800s. Cast iron; 11 individual pans connected in a frame. ¾"H., 12½"L., 8½"W., $55.00+.

Popovers Pan

Ca. 1890s. Also called the "Gem Pan" for dinner biscuits; cast iron; impr: GRISWOLD NO. 10, ERIE, PA. U.S.A. 940C. 11 spaces; popovers were made from a quick egg-rich bread batter that in baking would expand, "pop over" the edges of the cups. Double finger holds. $58.00+.

Cake Pan

Ca. 1890s. Gray tin; fluted sides. 2¾"H., 6"TD., $22.50.

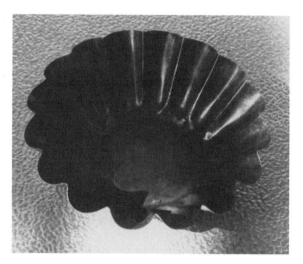

Muffin Pan

Ca. 1900s. Tin; fluted individual cake cups in a solid frame; stamped: EKCO, Pat. Pend. Chicago. Around 1929 the EKCO Company purchased A&J Mfg. Co., of Binghamton, N.Y., and produced varied forms of kitchenware for many years, retaining the initialed A&J diamond trademark until the mid–1900s. $15.00.

Baker/Griddle

Cast iron; for griddle cakes or thin pancakes to be rolled up with dessert or meat course centers; three individual sections; frame extended handholds; heavy wear signs. 15¾"L., 5"D., $22.50.

Swing Handle Basket

Ca. early 1800s. Shaker-style ribbed, woven oak splint; adaptation of Nantucket basket but without the pine bottom; demijohn (kicked-up) bottom, 1"W. carved handle and whittled wooden pins. 7½"H., 12"TD., 7½"BD., $395.00.

All Purpose Basket

Ca. 1800s. Carved oak handle held between double rims; New England origin – possibly Shaker made. 12"H., 8"D., $335.00.

Mending/Sewing Basket
Ca. mid–1800s. Also could be used for table service; splint weaving done in Floyd County, Georgia. 4¾"H., 10"TD., 7"BD., $125.00.

Farm Utility Basket
Ca. mid–1800s. Tall ash splint; no handle; bulbous with x-wrapped double rim and base; Maine origin. 8½"H., 8"TD., 6¾"BD., $165.00.

All Purpose Basket

Ca. 1870s. Woven oak splint; hard usage; every other rib tucked in between double rim; handle repaired with tape. 7"H., 17½"D., $135.00.

Buttocks Basket

Tightly woven oak splint; carved handle extends underneath; closely wrapped rim., $195.00.

Market Basket

Flat, squared double handles on loops to loosely swing; oak splint. 12½"H., 15"L., $175.00.

Market Basket

Ca. 1900s. Factory made; oak splint; nailed and stapled; one corner broken out; now used in a shelf display with damage turned to the rear. $45.00.

Gathering Basket

Woven oak splint; walnut hulls dyed bands; low handle held in the rim; flat bottom; Georgia origin. 13" to top of handle; 11"TD., $115.00.

Utility Basket

Ca. 1870, from Georgia. Handle continues down each side; woven oak splints. Popcorn berries. 5½"H basket only, 8"D. Baskets were essential in the kitchens along with so many other wares; for berrying, getting vegetables from the gardens, carrying lunches out to the fields, vittles home from the general store, for chunks of pone and biscuits at the eating table ... and more. $128.00.

Baskets

All ca. late 1800s–1900s. Measurements are to handle tops. All are miniatures, single rim wrappings. **General utility baskets** *(left and center). For gathering eggs, mending, etc.; Shaker style, both slant to squared bottoms. The darker is middle-bulbous. Left basket, 8"H., 6¼"TD; center basket, 7"H., 6¼"TD. Smallest basket is woven oak splint thought to have been made by the Seneca Indians. 5"H., 3½"W., $178.00 each.*

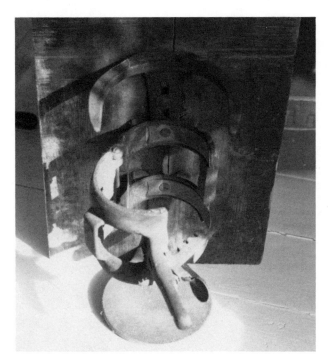

Asparagus Buncher

Cast iron, mounted on a pine slab; handle with its notches for bunch sizing brings clamps lightly around the fresh-cut stalks placed upright on the bottom iron plate, holds them for string tying; then the housewife carried them to market along with eggs, butter, or whatever she might sell that day. 8"H., 5"W., $128.00.

Deep Fryer Baskets/French Fryers

Ca. 1900–1930s. Both tinnned wire, one coarse and one finely meshed; wrapped rims plus straight and twisted handle portions; both table-rests during frying could be hooked over one rimside of the kettle, the handle lying on the other, which kept the frying contents from being scorched by touching the bottom of vessel. The top basket has an uncommonly large table rest stand and is the oldest of the two. 8"TD., $28.00. The bottom basket has slanted sides and coarser mesh and a smaller table rest. 8½"TD., $25.00.

Basket

Ca. 1900s. Shown folded flat as it stayed full length only when holding potatoes, greens, vegetables, whatever, for washing and/or acting as a temporary potato storage. Tinned double woven wire mesh; aluminum band. $22.50.

Combination Utensil/Worker

Ca. 1890s. Tin; screw-on top; arched side handle; stamped: A&J'S Mfg. Co., Binghamton, N.Y. in their diamond trademark; also marked: STRAINER, FRUIT JAR FILLER, FUNNEL, MEASURE, DIPPER. Popular with Pennsylvania Dutch cooks. $22.50.

Ricer

Ca. 1930s. Red painted wood, tin, zinc-plated iron; wood insert gives wire-frame handle better rigidity; for pressing cooked potatoes and the like through the base perforations, converting them into rice-like bits – this activated by handle-turning the smashing plate. $25.00.

Baker/Dutch Oven

Ca. late 1800s. Cast iron; taller lid affords higher baking space and place for steam; arc lid-lift; bail wire ends hook into double slot ears; wide tilt bar at back. 4½"H., 11"D., $65.00.

Bean Crocks/Pots

Ca. 1890s. Redware; light brown outside, deeper inside glazing; handles and lid knobs applied underglaze; GUERNSEY stamped on each base; upper New York State origin. This earthenware universally plentiful in American red clay deposits; from these pottery/crockery objects were made for everyday homewares (and dairies). Redware continued for about 200 years from our Colonial 1600s, produced in quantities, subject to minimal usage damage. Larger crock, 6½"H., 4¾"D; smaller crock, 4½"H., 3½"D., $125.00+.

Berry Bucket

Ca. 1800s. Gray speckled deeper granite; chipped rim; wire handle. 4⅛"H., 5¼"D., $78.00.

Kitchen Storage Vessel

Ca. 1700s. Hand fashioned from pine; used for whatever it was needed – apples, corn or cornmeal, and much more. New England origin. 15"H., 19¼"D., $225.00 – 250.00+.

Cornpone Pan

Ca. 1880. Original handle broken and this is a replacement; inside the pan are 12 raised lines in the iron casting with an "x" line at center, these to leave a pattern in the pone as it is inverted after baking/pan frying. 7"D., $85.00.

Milk Bowls

Ca. 1880. Both heavy pottery, rich brown glazed inside and out; flat bottoms; wide rims handy, to quote a farm wife, "to better hang onto a bowl when handling them in cooling milk." 5"H., 10"TD.; 4⅜"H., 8½"TD. $55.00 each.

Colander

Ca. Victorian 1800s. Majolica, rare in this form; 16 unevenly spaced drainage holes; three short fat feet; small no-harm rim repair. 2½"H., 11½"W., $225.00 – 250.00.

This piece is lead-glazed earthenware; Americans produced this principally in Maryland and Pennsylvania, possibly in other areas.

Colander

Ca. 1890s. Gray granite; overall perforated holes in alternately straight lines; strap-wide handles; foot-fast-base ring stand; the only wear is around the inside bottom ring. 12"TD., $58.00.

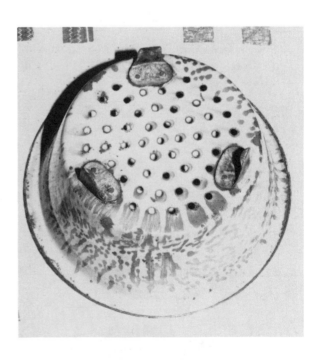

Colander

Shades of gray and white granite; bottom only shown to display its unusual wide low metal feet. 3½"H., 9"TD., $58.00.

Meat Roaster/Roasting Pan

Ca. late 1800s–1900. Pale robin's egg blue gran-
ite, a color sought by collectors, and, naturally,
values have increased; ridged sides; wire rings
control opening of two tin top steam-emission
vents in the lid half; four handles; emb: REED at
top center of lid. 9"H., 16½"L., $155.00.

Open Baking Pan

Gray speckled granite; shallow; wire han-
dles; edge wear; no holes. 10" square,
$45.00.

Scotch Bowl

Ca. 1890s. Black cast iron with sloping sides; later
wire handle; wire tilting ring; named for its cooking
thick barley soups and porridges; no lid required
as constant stirring was required to keep the
foods from sticking and scorching. 4½"H., 11¼"D.,
$38.00.

Cooking Pot

Ca. 1890s. Cast iron; tilting tab in the casting; dealer has for realism display substituted the only available piece in the booth that fits at all – a double pothook; values differ considerably to areas, size, and condition on these wares. $35.00.

Griddle

Ca. 1890s. Cast iron, for hot cakes and pancakes; also used as an omelet pan for omelets could be easily slipped off the shallow out-sloping sides. A Kentucky granny used it for years for cooking fried bread (French Toast). 8½"D., $38.00.

Tin Cup
Tinner-made with applied wide, center grooved handle. 2"H., 3"D., $10.00.

Breakfast Skillet
Cast iron, designed for bacon and eggs; base marked: WAGNER WARE, SIDNEY, O. NO. 11010. 9" square., $45.00.

Saucepan

Ca. 1860. Heavy copper; inside tinned; riveted cast iron handle and an opposite side handhold, the latter to make lifting or tipping this heavy cooking aid easier. 10"H., 21"L. handle, $395.00.

Spider

Ca. early 1800s. Cast iron newly blackened; uncommonly high legs; used in down hearth cookery; may have had a lid. $150.00.

Skillet

Ca. 1890s. Cast iron No. 5; pouring lips each side; known from the 1500s–1600s, skillets were first simply deep covered pans somewhat like porringers. A spider was a similar vessel, but with three legs that kept foods from burning if they were in any closer contact with the hearth heat. Then, gradually, the words somehow were combined. Skillets were and are still made in a number of sizes. $45.00.

Pail

Ca. 1800s. Two-toned gray granite; wire; wood; a few inside wear scars, no holes; lightly stained halfway up inside. Trademark on base: GRANITE IRONWARE. 6½"H., 6½"BD., $75.00.

Drinking Cup

Cobalt and white speckled granite; wide handle. 2¾"H., 3½"D., $25.00.

Pail

Ca. 1800s. Gray speckled cobalt granite; wire. 6⅝"H., 9"TD., $75.00+.

Rolls of striped ticking strips used for making rag rugs, etc. – for display only.

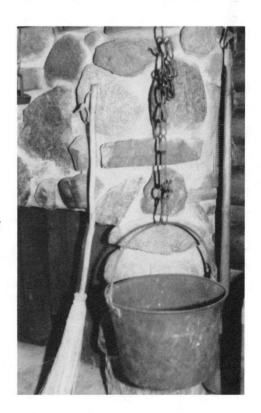

Pail

Ca. 1800s. Copper, iron bail with copper ears riveted; fairly new tangled chain. $145.00.

Fireplace/Yard Kettle

Ca. 1830–40. Cast iron; smaller size from Ohio frontier origin; bail gone; here set on a wrought iron **trivet** (ca. 1700s) for display; these hung on fireplace chains/cranes; weather permitting, could be used outdoors suspended from a sort of tripod or in a large basket-type iron frame; for cooking foods like applebutter, lard from tallows, and more. $165.00+.

Pail

Ca. 1800s. Cast brass; iron swing handle held by copper riveted ears; one inside soldered repair so small it is scarcely noticable; few dents. 8"H., 11½"TD., 8¾"BD., $125.00+.

Kettle

Same composition as pitcher described below; tip bar and squared handhold wire. 12½"TD., $45.00.

Pitcher

Pale blue and white granite; even though hard used and old, its bulbous curves and squarish handle have their own appeal; practical for holding flowers on a kitchen windowsill or on a counter holding wooden spoons. 5"TD., $55.00.

Custard Cup

Ca. 1890s. Brown outside and lighter inside glazed earthenware. 2½"H., ¾"D., $22.50.

Toy Skillet

Ca. 1910. Black painted cast iron; two sides pouring lip; be careful of these if you want an old one – they are heavily reproduced. $12.50.

Porringer

Ca. 1800s–early 1900s. Blackened iron, white granite inside; impr. on base: CLARK'S PATENT. 2½"H., 6¼"TD., $75.00.

Biscuit/Doughnut Cutters

Ca. 1930s. Aluminum, wood; smaller one is stamped on top: USE E Z BAKE FLOUR; 1½"H., 2½"D., $25.00. Larger one is 3¼"H., 1¼"D., $25.00. Doughnut cutters usually had a smaller round (for making the holes) that fit on the narrow collar seen inside as here.

Toy Pot and Lid

Ca. 1800s. Speckled white on cobalt; lid fits down into groove; base marked: ST. EL-WOOD. Trademark and Pat. date not legible. 3¼"H., 3"TD., $75.00.

Range Kettle/Pot

Ca. 1900. Stunning cobalt and gray granite; 3" wide iron up-and-down movable rimside attached bar/tilter emb: MAJESTIC. (Manufactured by the same company producing cookstoves "Great Majestic Ranges" at St. Louis, MO). With tilting devices the cooks could stand farther back from getting scalded by steam when emptying boiling contents. 8½"H., 13"TD., $195.00.

Kettle

Ca. 1900s. White granite; wire; one side has ring hook which probably held some sort of tilting device. 7½"H., 12½"TD., $55.00.

Scale

A rarity. Solid brass; etched L.E. BROWN'S PAT. DEC. 3, 1878; weight of food placed on the round platform turns it, at which point the attached slender long needle moves with it, stopping to show the weight on the larger circumference (shaft up from the base) since the weight units are etched on that upright. The needle stops at the correct weight – up to 12 lbs. Patterned with attractive lines; rolled bottom edges; also shown upside down to display the unusual design on the underside. Scales were important to housewives needing to check traders' supplies, or when "standing market" to be sure they gave their customers full value. 10¾"H., 9"TD., $275.00.

Utility Scale

Ca. 1900s. HANSON; white enameled base, black metal tray and fixtures. 25 lb. capacity; platform depresses under the food's weight; with spring action inside. $38.00.

"Handcuff" Scales

Ca. 1860. Cast iron, brass center; two hooks and a ring for hanging whatever smaller food item needed to be weighed; etched indicators – wts. 18 lbs. on one side, 15 lbs. on the other. Face 3½"D. The hook holding the scale is ca. 1800; wrought iron, straight and twisted stem, rat tail curved both ends. $165.00+.

Spring Balance Scales

Ca. 1800s–1900s. Chicken scales in some areas. Kitchen essentials, they performed regularly; old recipes might call for ingredients in pounds or ounces; the traveling Huckster may have forgotten his scales – or needed to be checked again; foods could be placed in baskets and hung from the rings or hooks; to sell one of her hens, a housewife tied its two legs together and hung it head-down – vigorously squawking – finally getting the weight. All these are of iron with one side brass, faces marked for poundage.

The two scales on the left are each CHATTILON IMPROVED, New York City & Penn., 50 lbs., 6"L., $55.00 each. The center one is black japanned DETECTO, New York, U.S.A., 100 lbs., 11"L., $55.00. Second from right is dark gray EXCELSIOR, Belmont Hdwe Co. U.S.A., 25 lbs., 5½"L., $45.00. Right is EXCELSIOR IMPROVED, Belmont Hdwe Co U.S.A., 10 lbs., brass, 4¼"L., $35.00.

Fireless Cooker Pan

Ca. early 1900s. Steam-cooked foods, especially meats, when pan was set down in bottom of open wells, all part of a tin-lined portable wood box (or metal) with, usually, three or four wells, having a heavy lid. Needing no fuel, it was a big safety factor, the pans sat on hot soapstone discs that had been heated; they kept the stove heat out of a kitchen, didn't need watching, and food was delicious. 5¼"H., 7½"D., $38.00.

Steamer/Cooker

Ca. 1903. Gray tin; one of four or five stacked sections side-fastened with four slides; strap handles and arched lid lift; when over hot water, steam rose through the center opening; a shelf inside each tier held the food; cone lid vent gave more space for boiling; a space saver for cookery labeled: THE HUNT COOKER, Patented Jan. 20, 1903, W.S. HUNT, OWOSSO, MICH. 15"H., 11"TD., $35.00.

Double Boiler

White swirls on pale blue granite; two parts; cobalt handle; inside scarring. Lost its lid. 6¾"H., $75.00.

Teakettle

Ca. 1800s. Iron cast in two sections joined at center; short bar thumb latch opens the lid; wire bail could be replacement. $195.00+.

"Putting By"

...for daily and winter meals

Food Crock/Sealing Wax Jar

Ca. 1880. Bulbous hand-thrown brown glazed earthenware; a few expected minor imperfections in this software; impr: JASPER ANDREW BISHOP 1836–1923. Locally known as "Dite Bishop," he was a potter in "Kenzie" (short for McKenzie), also a store owner in the Jugtown area of Pike/Upson Counties, Georgia. 9"H., 5½"D., $165.00 – 175.00.

Crock

Ca. 1890. Glazed white stoneware, brown inside; cobalt decorated with flower and cactus; impr: E.S. & B. NEW-BRIGHT, PA. 12"TD., 10"BD., $250.00 – 275.00.

Housewives found these wares scarce as the clay was not universally found and transportation costs were high. Arrival of the Erie Canal and better roads quickly accelerated building of new potteries and availability for purchasing increased.

Crocks

Ca. 1850s. Both impr: J.F. FISHER & CO. LYONS, N.Y.; on the smaller the name is brushed on in the center of curlicues. 11½"H., 8"TD., 5¼"BD. The larger crock has a two-gallon capacity; brushed-on cobalt leaves and a dark brown inside glaze. 9¼"H., 9¾"D., $195.00 – 225.00.

Crock

Ca. 1870. Stoneware; brushed-on cobalt leaves; two-gallon capacity; close-set handles. These ovoid shapes didn't balance well when stacked in kilns nor in shipping containers. Gradually, straight sides replaced the bulbous styles. 10"H., 9"TD., 7"BD., $125.00 – 150.00.

Canning Jar

Ca. 1800s. In cobalt letters: FORT EDWARD STONEWARE CO., FORT EDWARD, N.Y. (near Lake George); one-gallon capacity; inside dark brown glaze; had a fit-down-in lid held by sealing wax; tight ears. 8½"H., 5½"TD., 6¾"BD., $125.00 – 150.00.

Preserves Jar

Ca. early 1800s. Sealing wax lid style; glaze named for that originally used by Albany Glass Co., Albany, N.Y., re-established in 1792, in operation until the 1820s; small rim chip. 6"H., 4¼"D., $55.00+.

Pickle Crock

Ca. 1870. Saltglazed stoneware, brown inside; cheesecloth or such was placed over the top (string or ragstrip tied under the rim for that purpose) of raw cucumber pickles, for instance, curing in brine, with pickling spices tied up in a cloth bag and laid among them. 11½"H., 8¼"D., $150.00 – 175.00.

Crocks

Very old; figures and crown with trademark: E. SWASEY & CO. U.S.A. on glazed brown and white stoneware.

One gallon – 7"H., 7⅞"TD., $125.00.
Two gallon – 8⅞"H., 10⅛"TD., $150.00.
Three gallon – 10⅜"H., 11"TD., $175.00.
Five gallon – 12½"H., 12½"TD., $195.00.

Fruit Canner/Sealing Wax Jar

Blown in a mold; two-quart size; tin airtight closure held by hot sealing wax poured into the recess around the tin to preserve contents; (when ready to serve the food, the hardened wax is cracked off, perhaps by lightly tapping with the wooden handle of a kitchen knife or such – and the lid is lifted with the knife's point – it gives a "squoosh" if properly pressure-kept); emb: STAR GLASS CO., NEW ALBANY, IND., $125.00+.

Crock

Fully glazed stoneware; the brown has run down into a "turkey eye" drip considered with favor by collectors; no chips. 5¼"H., 7½"TD., $75.00 – 95.00.

Jug

Ca. 1700s. Stoneware glazed inside and out; two-gallon; squiggles in cobalt; a far northern dealer said that earlier, in her rural counties at least, housewives liked to paint such jugs to brighten their kitchens – or even match newly colored woodwork – that when dealers bought the jugs for shop sales, they had to remove the paint – a hard job; impr. above the design: FISHER, LYONS, N.Y. 14¾"H., 2½"TD open mouth, $295.00+.

Food Crock

Ca. 1880. Earthenware outside glaze with darker lettering and design, inside deeper glaze; two gallon; WILLIAMS & HOPPERT, GREENSBORO, PA. 12¼"H., 7½"TD., $375.00.

Storage Jar

Ca. 1800s – early 1900s. Glazed inside and out stoneware; turned wood on wire handle; flat button lid lift; stored mincemeat, brandied fruits, pickles and the like – whatever – to be removed in quantities as needed; these were convenient for the cooks who couldn't run to the trading post for a can of something for supper; mint condition. 9½"H., 7¾"TD., 9"BD., $95.00 – 125.00.

Batter Jug

Ca. late 1800s. For pancakes, waffles, etc.; clear glazed stoneware, brown glazed inside, no lid; wire drop-bail affixed each end to "bosses"; wood grip; the big ears, base tilt bar (hollow underneath), and rim better accommodated fingers for this was heavy when filled; large spout which originally probably had a tin cover as so many did; bulbous shape is impr: A. FARRINGTON, ELMIRA, N.Y. In 1882 A. Farrington established a pottery at Elmira, operating under the ownership of "father and son" until 1895 – one of the few potteries in New York State to have been owned throughout its history by specially-trained potters. 10"H., 5½"TD., 6¾"BD., $175.00+.

Jug

Ca. 1910. White below, brown top and interior glazed stoneware impr: C. PERSON'S SONS, BUFFALO, N.Y.; probably for ownership security someone later added the "P"; originally had a cork (easily replaceable) which kept contents safe. 12"H., 7"BD., $75.00+.

Salt Crock

Ca. late 1800s. Glazed inside and out; curved inside base makes reaching in for a pinch of salt convenient; the cook might sharpen her knives on the edges for a quick cutting need. 3¾"H., 6"D., $45.00.

Canning Jar

Both colors clear glazed; iron wire fixtures lock together the lid onto the jar (off-kelter trying to get the photo); snaps in reverse to open; lid emb: PAT. MAR. 1, 1882. 6"H., 3½"D., $65.00+.

Jug

Ca. 1800s. Saltglazed stoneware; emb: BUFFALO, N.Y.; large underglaze handle; thick-rimmed narrow mouth; held eating-table and cooking liquids such as vinegar, molasses, anything the cook wanted to put in it to use as she needed it. 14"H., $150.00+.

Thrown into a kiln when it was at peak temperature, warmed common table salt vaporized, giving the stacked forms a clear shiny glaze, sealing the clay, making it ideal for ktichen usages. (Fusing often resulted in a deposit of "orange peel" – throwing in cider ash left rougher tiny sharp bumps.)

Jug

Ca. 1800s. Hard used but no holes, only scarring; bottom impr: LANCASTER CTY, PENN.; note blending of underglaze handle into small mouth; hand throwing rings attractive. 14¾"H., 9"BD., $125.00 – 145.00.

Redware Jug

Ca. early 1800s. Shiny glaze inside and out on red clay; northwestern N.Y. State origin; chubby rolled rim and a rare large grooved and graceful handle. 11"H., 27" around bulbous middle, $225.00 – 250.00.

Jugs

Ca. 1800s. Both brown shiny glazed stoneware from a New England pottery; made in two sections, then joined. The taller one has a rim of natural light clay at joining of the two parts; signed "A." 12"H., 6¾"BD., $95.00+. The smaller one has a wavy pouring lip above a narrow throat; again the very large graceful handle, and concentric lines for decoration. 9½"H., 9"BD., $125.00+.

Pantry Boxes

Ca. 1800s. Both bentwood with nailed laps; each is lid-signed WILDER R. CLARK. Large, 6"H., 10"D., $120.00. Small, 6"H., 4½"D., $110.00.

Pantry Box

Ca. 1800s–1900. Oak bentwood; faded green paint; nailed. 4¾"H., 7½"D., $65.00 – 75.00.

Circular wood boxes during the 1700s and 1800s held large cheeses, spices, herbs, seeds, and a number of foods. The colonists usually had iron handcut nails; Shakers used innumerable boxes but they preferred copper nails on pointed finger laps. Maple boxes might have pine tops and bottoms.

"Treenware" meaning "of trees"covers virtually all types of kitchenware, made by the colonists/settlers themselves or by village coopers, since that raw material was so plentifully close at hand and wore well. Utensils/containers for preparing, serving, and storing foods were used, especially by those moving on into unsettled regions – and into later years by rural folks – handcarved, turned on a foot lathe, or with hand tools, very little signed. In the 1800s bowls in New England were sometimes painted with homemade colors to preserve and brighten them. In the 1800s metal wares and factory produced pottery items grew more widely available, although on the far frontiers, treenware continued to be made for a number of years. Small boxes of wood, tin, or leather stored "things," particularly in one-room living; holding everything from precious buttons to foods and trinkets. Often those that held brown sugars, herbs, roots, spices, and such can be identified by sniffing; in others there may be a tiny thread of old lace or a faded old recipe.

Herb Box

Ca. 1900. Bentwood; early nails; wire bail with tin keepers; from a top color variance, it probably originally had a lid. 3¼"H., 9¼"D., $55.00 – 65.00.

Lidded Herb Box

Ca. 1800s. Bentwood; old nails; mouse attempted entry at top of lid band. 6"H., 9¼"D., $125.00.

Sugar Bucket

Ca. mid–1800s. All original; staved butternut; good mustard yellow paint; carved
wood handle pinned to the sides; button
knob on lid; smithy forged nails hold the
bentwood wrappings. 9½"H., 10"D.,
$175.00 – 195.00.

Sugar Firkin

Ca. 1800s. Pine; staved oak; copper tacks
hold lapped-over bentwood bands – stain
suggests there may have been a third band
above the one at bottom; carved handle
wood-pinned at lapovers; underside of lid
impr: F. LANE & SON, MARLBORO DEPOT.
14"H., 14½"TD., $195.00 – 225.00.

Sugar Firkin

Ca. 1860. Staved wood with peg-fastened
carved handle and bands; marked: WILD-
ER & SON, SOUTH BINGHAM, MASS.
10½"H., 9"D., $195.00 – 225.00.

Sugar Cutter

Very old; handmade to an ingenious idea from pine; signed by the maker: A. Hollins; four corners are large dovetailed; a black iron hinged lift lid; inside is a one-end hinged sharp steel blade with a wood handle and brass ferrule, for strengthening and to prevent splitting of the wood; this handle, pulled forcibly down onto a block of sugar already set on the iron slab slices the cone's sides; this cuts off particles from the chunk or pulverizes the solid sweets; the released sugar bits drop through the big-bored holes into the shallow drawer below. Opened by its wire brass ring pull, the drawer is pulled out and emptied of its contents. Thought to have been made for the white refined kind known as "basin sugar," intended for tea table guests and at more affluent dining room tables. $250.00 – 295.00.

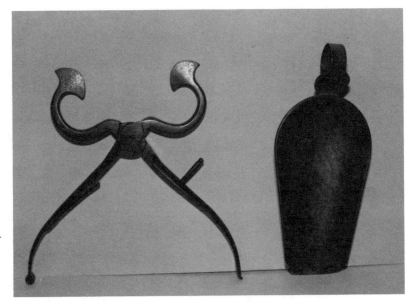

Sugar Nippers

Ca. 1800s. Polished cast iron; spring handle (folded up here in the picture against one handle); cleaver's sharp cutters snipped pieces off tea sugar (refined white customarily bought in indigo-blue wrapped paper the housewife could use for dyes); particularly in one-room kitchen living, then in servants's eating kitchens, bowls of coarse ground or snipped brown sugar known as basin sugar were on tables along with salt and pepper. One handle has a hand rest; one handle end is curled much more than the other, coming together the more elaborate end was on top. About 8"H., $165.00 – 175.00.

Sugar Scoop

Ca. 1800s. Black tin; generous strap handle. 7½"L., $45.00.

Canisters

Japanned blue and white tin; white porcelain knobs held with brass screws; COPYRIGHT 1916 VENDOME CO. 110 EAST 16TH ST. NEW YORK USA; larger tins contained as labeled – Tea, Sugar, Coffee, Rice, Barley; smaller tins held Cinnamon, Pepper, Nutmeg, Allspice, Cloves, and Ginger. 3¾"H to 6"H., $245.00 set.

Canisters

Ca. late 1890s. Japanned black tin; original lovely bronzed designs now dimmed beyond seeing exact patterns; lids are released by lifting small tabs. The two larger ones are 7"H., 5½"D. With Coffee and Tea in the larger tins, six spice cans fit into the handled carrying box. Metal containers best prevented invasions of weevils and mice. $95.00 – 125.00 set.

Scoop

Ca. 1890. Black tin; uncommon rest bar; rolled rim and scoop shovel part lines trimmed. 10¼"L., $55.00 – 75.00.

While we usually accredit these to sugar, they might also have been used to scoop meal or other dry ingredients as there is no stain evidence; wire loop.

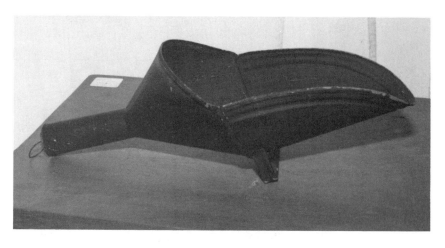

Sugar Jar
Ca. 1920s. Thick two-mold bulbous-sided pressed glass, flat oblong base; tin lid. 8½"H., 5"TD., $45.00.

Sugar Scoop
Ca. late 1800s. Handmade from tin; lapped joints; soldered on handle. 2⅞"L., 1⅞"W., $10.00.

Butter & Egg Money Box

Ca. 1800s. Today resides on a kitchen shelf in a kitchen in New York State's Lake Ontario region just as it sat long ago in a Canadian kitchen across the lake. Made from pine; in original mustard yellow script it is signed by the maker: C.A. OHLHEIS, WALKERTON, ONT.; a carriage painter at Ontario, Canada before 1867. In side grooves its sliding top has cutouts for opening at either end; historical and still practical. $45.00.

Spice Canister

Early; tin; six sections; center is for round nutmeg grater; marked: BUNCOME COUNTY, N.C. $75.00+.

Family Cash Box

Ca. 1800s–1900s. Dark stained poplar; iron keepers; wire latch; kept hidden back of crocks on a high kitchen shelf for monies to be dropped through the slot, a little at a time, from the housewife's sale of eggs, butter, etc. – taken out and counted on Saturday nights at the eating table; (may have originally been made for a store purpose but so far as we know, it has been in a home for a long time.) $38.00.

Cook's Utility Box

The general store owner at the crossroads may have given it away once the original contents had been sold; found in a kitchen at an estate sale; there is black print: ESTABLISHED 1780; a bakerwoman wearing a mobcap (frills, full crown, fastened under her chin) carries a tray; also reads: GOLD MEDAL AWARDED PARIS EXPOSITION 1900; WALTER BAKER & CO., LTD, DORCHESTER, MASS. Pine, dovetailed four corners. 7½"H., 10¼"W., 7¼"DP., $125.00 – 145.00.

Biscuit Box

Ca. early 1900s. Tin; traces of white, black, and green japanned paints; lid is stamped with a ship; sides have ship pictures including The Scotia 1862, City of Rome 1884, Mauritania 1907, Majestic reconditioned 1921, The Great Eastern 1858; made in England and carried or sent here as a gift; after its first contents (cookies/biscuits) were eaten, it brightly graced a shelf of an American northeast coastal kitchen, still keeping pastry treats fresh – and free from ambitiously exploring rodents. 3⅛"H., 5¼"W., 7"L., $55.00.

Kilderkin/Rundlet

Ca. 1820–40. Maple; also made from hollowed-out tree trunks, copper – and cypress in the south; to hold around 18 gallons of liquid; used both for home storage and at inn kitchens. Farm housewives could use them for sending cooling drinks of water or fruit drinks to the fieldhands on hot days. 8½"H., 5½"D., $225.00 – 250.00.

Baking Powder Cans

Ca. 1910. Tin; lids emb: CALUMET 1 lb. BAKING POWDER, ABSOLUTELY PURE. Particularly in more remote sections, housewives bought staples in larger quantities than townsfolk needed to keep on hand. 5⅞"H., 3"D., $25.00 each.

Barrel

Ca. 1800s. Staved wood, nailed bands; Frontier settlers carried these in covered wagons; later kept in early kitchens holding white flour if it was available or anything else the cook stored; today it still stands in a kitchen holding various non-perishable items. 30⅝"H., 15"D. $150.00 – 175.00.

At the Eating Table

Table Utensils Box

Ca. 1800s. Hand fashioned from pine; all original; black japanned; end carrying slots; divided spaces to carry sugar bowl, salt and pepper shakers, any eating utensils – whatever was needed in setting the table for a meal fit into this steps-saver. 4"H., 10⅝"L., 6¾"W., $135.00 – 175.00.

Utensils Box

Ca. early 1800s. Handmade "on the place" in south Georgia; blue painted soft wood; nice big carrying slot. 4¾"H., 10"L., $150.00.

Table Utensils Box

Ca. 1920s. Handcarved; white showing through mustard-yellow painted pine. 4½"H., 12"L., 7⅞"W., $75.00 – 95.00.

Utensils Box

Ca. 1800s. Handmade form local Florida pine; wide hand-curved carrier slot. 3¼"H., 11½"L., 9"W., $125.00 – 150.00.

Utility Box

Ca. 1800s. Displayed on center of a kitchen table; original green paint is scarred; old smithy-forged nails; ½" thick sides. 5¼"H., 29"L., $95.00 – 125.00.

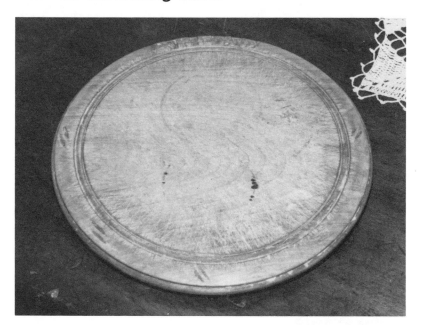

Bread Cutting/Serving Plate

Ca. 1920s. Wood, rim design; beveled edge; soft patina; minute cutting marks. 9¾"D., $55.00.

Bread Cutting/Serving Plate

Ca. 1930s. Wood; beveled edge; emb: FLETCHER'S SUPER BAKERY; patina feels oily; center worn lower from habit of loaves held in the same position when sliced; overall tiny shallow cuts. 10"D., $58.00 – 65.00.

Bread Knife

Ca. 1890s. Wood; carbon steel. 14"L., $38.00.

Bread Cutting Tray/Server

Ca. 1920s. Maple; carved feather design on edge; covered with light cutting marks; noted on these softwood kitchen pieces, center is worn thinner from loaf of bread being held at the same place to be cut. 12"D., $55.00.

Birthday Cake Board

Ca. 1920s. Maple; stamped on bottom: "Pat. appld for." Candle holder spaces at edges, two lines bored offset to better space the candles. 14"D., $50.00.

Butter Bucket

Pale gray speckled granite; cobalt handle; brass riveted ears each side and wide curled lid lift; concentric lines trim the body; different and appealing. This was filled with butter, kept in a cool place, then at mealtime set right on the kitchen table. 8"H., 8¾"L., 6"W., $125.00+.

Beer Bucket/Pail

Ca. early 1900s. Tin; half gallon size; concentric lines for decoration; wire bail and lid ring; also called a table pail. As supper was about ready to be set on the table, the man went down to a corner gathering-place (saloon) where for a nickel the pail was filled with cold beer. Carried home, it was set on the table and mugs and glasses filled. $35.00.

Ale Bucket

Ca. 1910. Wire handle and ring lid lifter; copper; gracefully curved sides; wear signs but no dents or damage. 6"H., 6"TD., 6½"BD., $95.00.

Rockingham Dishes

Ca. 1800s–early 1900s. Mottled light brown and darker marbled glazed compact earthenware sometimes known as Tortoise Shell. Made in America from the early 1800s by Norton & Fenton, the finest Vermont potters. The chocolate brown or red-brown glazes originated in the Staffordshire District at Rockingham, England, ca. 1790s. It became a universal name for hundreds of similar glazes, sometimes confused with Bennington. Note that stack marks have age-bled through the glaze on one dish – it may even have bled into the glaze when drying. $295.00+ set.

2"H., 8½"W., 10⅜"L.
2"H., 7¾"W., 9½"L.
1¾"H., 7"W., 8¾"L.

Bone Dishes

Ca. 1887. Semi porcelain, scalloped edges; both were white but one became darker tinged with age as earthenwares will do; these were almost standard equipment on eating tables far into the 1900s, especially in rural regions, customarily shared by two individuals as receptacles for cleaned-off bones after hungry appetites had consumed the good meaty parts. 6"L., 3"W., $18.00 set.

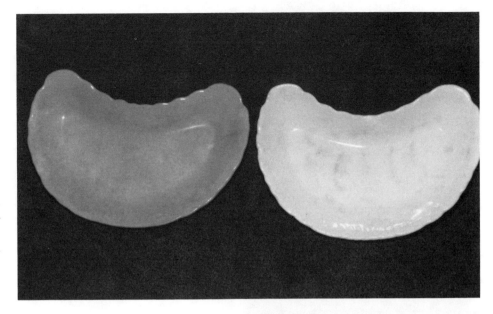

Master Salt

Ca. 1800s. Pewter. 2⅓"H., 2½"D., $65.00+.

Fruit/Utility Bowl

Ca. 1880. Sponge-dabbed white earthenware with cobalt; glazed inside and out; pewter base ring. 7"H., 11"TD., $250.00 – 275.00.

Plate

Ca. 1800s. Pewter; LONDON mark on bottom but other marks too worn to identify. In checking value, dealer stated it would sell for about $75.00, but since it had been so shabbily treated with many scars, it sold for about $10.00. 9½"D., $10.00.

Child's Plate
Gray and white granite. 7"D., $15.00.

Dinner Plate
Gray mottled white granite. 8¾"D., $18.00.

Children's Dishes

Ca. 1900s. White and cobalt granite; hinged lid, acorn finial teapot, 4¼"H., 8½"Round; five cups; two plates each 8½"D, others 6¼"D. and 4½"D., $45.00.

Fly Screen/Food Protector

Ca. 1870s. Japanned tin; wire ring and very fine mesh. 15½"D., $28.00.

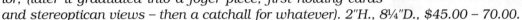

Tray/Server

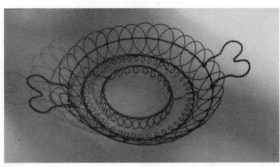

Ca. late 1800s–1900. Lacy looped twisted wire dish generally having a painted porcelain plate down inside (dear to Victorian hearts – some interlaced theirs with ribbons); this dish, 3rd generation same family usage, in which tea cookies and such pastries were taken from the kitchen into the parlor; (later it graduated into a foyer piece, first holding cards and stereoptican views – then a catchall for whatever). 2"H., 8¼"D., $45.00 – 70.00.

Wireware, a basic essential to American pioneers, has been used for making kitchenware items since our first 13 colonies. Wire, known in the 3rd millenium B.C., metal strips of sheet metal shaped with hand tools; gradually refining the processes, by the latter 1200s, European wire workers kept pulling strips (which took a lot of physical strenghth) through smaller and smaller holes in metal plates called dies or drawplates, striving to reach certain gauges. Finally, from 1831 when a blacksmith began an ultimate improvement, wire manufacturers in the latter 1800s were able to easily and commercially-inexpensively produce innumerable items in desired gauges.

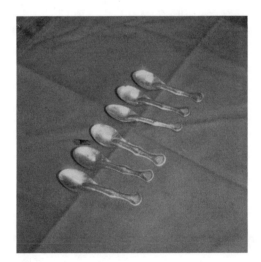

Dessert Spoons

Ca. 1900s. Stamped tin; grooved handles; type also familiar at some soda and ice cream parlors. 4" to 5"L., $5.00.

Fork

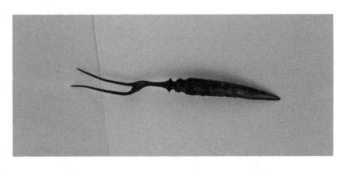

Ca. late 1700s–1800. North Carolina origin; deer horn handle; one tine bent from age and regular usage. Knife blades – sharp bayonet points ontapered handles – stabbed the foods, points carrying pieces or chunks to mouths. Mainly used for serving, two-tined small forks appeared in the late 1500s, three or four tines made by the 1700s. However, two-tined ones were made and used throughout 1800s Victoriana. In the 1600s, they accompanied many owners when dining out since they were so highly valued as personal property; used at other than home tables, when the meal was over, they were pocketed again to be taken home. Forks gradually supplanted fingers and knives as eating utensils. $38.00.

Trencher

Ca. early 1800s. Handcarved from one piece of pine; wide end rims for holding and keeping food contained; good wear marks with no imperfections; a plate from which to eat, a platter on which to serve and/or carve. (A "trencherman" was generally known as a "hearty eater.") 4"H., 21¾"L., 14½"W., $165.00 – 175.00+.

Table Forks

Ca. 1890s. Wood, steel; three tines (prongs); three rivets hold two wood handle pieces together with the tines continued between them for rigidity. Made from woods, bone, and steel, there were at least a hundred different patterns. Plain, 7"H.; inlaid, 7¼"H., $25.00 each.

Trencher

Ca. 1830–40. Handcarved from one piece of pine; could be used to serve food but this was more often for a one-dish meal, piled with a mixture of meal, vegetables, rice, and other avail-

able foods, for instance, from which a family seated around the table scooped out portions with spoons the settler had carved. In various early slaves' cabins, more primitively carved trenchers had food mixtures carried to mouths with fingers or wood slivers as the utensils. One side is worn down, perhaps from a cook hitting a spoon there to shake off clinging morsels. 20"L., $150.00+.

Coffeepot

Tinned copper, wood in a shaped, turned handle and posts; acorn finial; extended back-lid thumb press to lift for adding freshly-ground coffee and water to the pot; (some cooks dropped in an egg to "clear" the brew); half-top pouring spout lid; copper ferrules. Was set on the eating table for refills. 7½"H., 3"TD., 4½"BD., $65.00.

Table Pan

(Since this appears in the same photo as the table coffee pot, we will put it also in that category – and who knows, it may easily have served as a dish on early tables short on conventional serving containers); speckled cobalt granite; also this shallow type was used for cooling down milk fresh from the cows. 2"H., 8½"TD., $25.00.

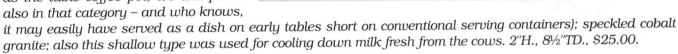

Coffeepot

Ca. later 1800s. Boldly patterned gray and white granite – looks like tiger skin gracefully shaped; note acorn finial on high convex lid; handle wedge for better comfort; well preserved; this piece must have been proudly sitting on the eating table. 9½"H., 4"TD., $135.00+.

Teakettle

Ca. late 1800s. Pale blue speckled granite on cast iron; hinged top that slides sideways has a missing finial; end of wood grip on wire the spout. 9½"H., 4"TD., $65.00.

Sugar Bowl

Ca. 1900s. Gray granite; bulbous with suitably-sized ears; probably had an original lid now missing; matches fairly well with the pot. 4"H., $45.00.

Coffeepot

Ca. 1900s. Speckled gray granite; large spout; acorn finial knob on rounded convex lid; note handle-handy shaping. This one was set right on the kitchen eating table for refilling cups at mealtime. (Remnants of the midday food were set in a pie safe or such to be kept as the basis for supper. Sometimes left right on the table, they were covered with a thin type of material such as cheesecloth, etc.) 7"H., 3¾"TD., 5¼"BD., $138.00 – 145.00.

Plate

Ca. 1900s. Gray granite; canted sides; this one was used at the table for one of the children, but it could double for a pie baking pan. 6"TD., 4"BD., $18.00.

Sugar Box

Ca. 1700s. Two-piece handsome treenware rarity; all original; mustard yellow color softly worn; no scarring; trim lines; tightly fitting center-recessed lid; (may have been used to hold salt as well at some other time); a collectible mighty hard to resist. 5½"H., 9½"D., $250.00 – 275.00.

Muffineer/Sifter

Ca. 1910. For flour or sugar with cinnamon, etc.; black tin; unevenly punched holes; wide strap handle. 3½"H., 3"D. Muffineers were also made of wood, pewter, glass, and pottery, dating from the 1600s – perhaps even earlier – shaker-top punched vessels to dust sugar on muffins; also used with spices or salt. 3½"H., 3"D., $48.00.

Mug
White granite; dealer said it is also called a "miner's mug"; wide man-sized handle. 4¼"H., 5"D., $35.00.

Sugar Bowl
White granite; fat around the middle; big stick-out handles; round knob-top lid. 6¼"H., $38.00.

Teapot

Ca. 1914-1918. Tinned metal nicely designed with attached small clips and turn slots to doubly hold it to a "stand" 4⅝"D. The "pot" is very thick (¼") emerald glass blown in a mold, with a polished pontil at center bottom; there is a tiny rounded pouring lip ½" length; its base is 3½"D. Tea prepared herein by the mess cook in a German field kitchen somewhere in Europe was given to the officer-owner, who could then carry it about with him for sipping, or set it on a field camp table to enjoy more leisurely. Brought into American Delaware after WWI, about 25 years ago it was purchased by a Floridian who, carefully preserving it, periodically washed and lightly oiled the tin, thus avoiding rust. A conversational heritage addition to any present-day kitchen. $225.00+.

Teapot

Ca. Late 1700s–1800. Handcrafted copper; wrapped seams with a few light hammer marks; overall fluting – note spout; wood lid knob and turned grip with copper ferrules on a fancifully-shaped copper-coated heavy iron handle; two parts joined near the base. 11"H., 6"D., $195.00.

Teakettle

Ca. early 1800s. Hand fashioned copper; squared strap type handle; hammer marks around the rim band; note snake-like shaping of heavy spout. 11"H., 6"TD., $135.00+.

Tea Ball

Tiny meshed wire full ball in a tin frame hinged at bottom and held at top by the chain keeper; filled with dried tea leaves (or sassafras – whatever was desired); the ball could be briefly dipped into a glass (Scandinavian style) or cup, but this size was customarily put down into a pot of hot water, chain dangling over outside, lid replaced, and tea could be steeped to desired color and flavor. 6"L., $15.00.

Nature's Bounties

. . . And speaking of milk, a curious milch cow in a Georgia pasture was pleased to model for us – from a distance. A bolder friend, wanting to share the limelight, wandered up to the fence and as we took the picture, got set to protest our presence with a vigorous "moooo!"

With the understanding that the following are all butter churns, they will be further identified as merely "churns."

Churn

Ca. early 1800s. Oak and maple; rare size; bought at a museum's auction; staved wood; brass rivets fasten black iron bands; cast iron fixtures; the exposed gear's shaft penetrates the lid; turning the handle causes two sets of paddles to agitate the cream into butter bits. 6½"H., 6"D., $375.00+.

Churn

Ca. 1870–1900. Pine; Amish owned; complete and original; cast iron handle with red knob is cream agitator; emb. on handle: THE BLANCHARD CHURN; squared base-tapered legs; inside horizontal paddles can be removed for scraping off butter bits and for cleaning. 33½"H., 22½"W., $295.00.

Cylinder Churn

Ca. mid 1890s. Printed: NEW STYLE WHITE CEDAR CYLINDER CHURN; three-gallon capacity; MADE IN U.S.A.; hoops are galvanized iron; wood grip handle; wingnut turned to release paddles; thumb and finger slots carved in lid. 15"H., 12½"D., 9¾"DP., $165.00.

Rocking Churn

Ca. 1900. Staved wood; handle grip with ferrule; cast iron fixtures; shaped as a keg or small barrel and fits into slots that permit swinging back and forth for churning. 33"H., $165.00.

Churn

Made in many shapes and sizes, these were all made for agitating cream into butter. Wood; cast iron fixtures; handle rocker; inside paddles activated; thick wood lid with lift-bar turned to open for up to 10-gallon capacity filling – turned in reverse closes and locks. Printed: MANUFACTURED BY R.W. FENNER, SOUTH STOCKTON, CHATAUQUA, N.Y. 39"H., 24" at peak, $250.00 – 275.00+.

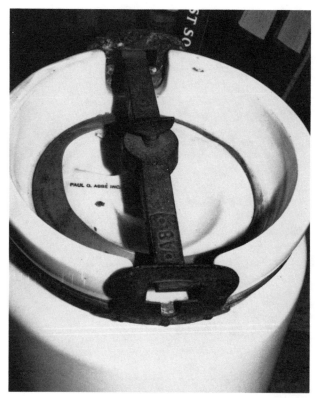

Churn

Ca. late 1800s. Glazed stoneware inside and out; black cast iron fixtures; printed on deeply recessed lid: PAUL O. ABBE´; Arkansas farm origin; wide rubber ring to prevent splashing; windmill activated attachments no longer available; as the windmill wheel turned in the wind, small (game-size) marble balls were tossed about – churning up the cream contents into butter; turning the large wingnut released the lid for taking out the butter and cleaning the container and marbles. 10"H., 8¼"TD., $125.00 – 150.00.

Churn

Ca. 1890s. White glazed stoneware; wood handle and dasher paddles; lift-ears; spatter-proof cup; potter's dimly seen initial "G" in blue; with dasher out, to protect the milk if she was not quite ready to churn, the housewife could add a cheesecloth cover tied with a string or rags under the wide rim – or if the cream has already been churned and she wanted to leave it in the churn awhile, she could also add the cover. 16"H., $148.00.

Churn

Ca. early 1800s. Up 'N Down dasher type; red stain; original and complete; wood and metal with shallow nails so the metal could not penetrate the staves, contaminating contents; upright is for easier handling. 19½"H., 10½"TD., $195.00.

Churn

Ca. 1800s. Salt glazed brown stoneware; uncommon two handles making for easier churn handling; finger-lift bar on opposite side; wooden lid; dasher and paddles are gone, but shouldn't be too difficult to replace as more churns than dashers were broken and thrown away; note the potter crookedly "threw" the rim – makes this a more unusual collectible. 17½"H., 8½"TD., $125.00 – 145.00.

Churn

Ca. 1850–70. White stoneware base; cobalt design; glazed brown lid and splatter cup; dasher not in the churn but is available; impr: F. WOODWORTH, BURLINGTON, VT. 16½"H to rim, $385.00.

Cream Skimmer/Cheater

Ca. 1890. Worn, showing some weather-exposure; pierced holes; held by hand at the rolled edge extension; it was for skimming the cream off the top of the milk – and perhaps less often – grease formed on soups, etc.; held with a cloth for cooked foods as heat could make this utensil too hot to handle without padding. $10.00.

Churn

Ca. 1800s. Heavy gauge tin; wide strap handles; wood dasher with holes bored paddles at the in-churn end; maple lid fits down on an inside groove. $225.00.

Churns

Ca. 1895–1900. All pressed glass; bulbous sides with vertical line designs; wood paddles intact; two grips are red and one green, with cast iron gear covers painted to match; tin screw tops ventilated about 1"L. tiny diameter holes. $95.00 – 125.00.

From our most northern borders to the tip of Florida. Prices on these in shops and at auctions, when seen, and in good condition, have a variance of as much as $50.00.

Churn

Ca. 1900s. Squared pressed glass; wood; screw tin top; cast iron fixtures; exposed gears; no chips. 13½"H., 5½" Square, $75.00.

Cream Separator

Ca. 1920s. Manufactured by McCormick Deering; complete and near-mint; about 30 spinners separate cream and milk, cream coming out at the top, skimmed milk at the bottom; removable varied-size round plates hold buckets or crocks for cream or milk; tinned steel wire-held mesh at top stops any insects or other foreign matter falling into the contents; if the wood handle is too slowly turned, a bell rings; when required turnings at 60 revolutions a minute are reached, centrifugal force silences the bell; the large top well of this white and black cast iron boon lifts off for access to cleaning each part the milk touches; the wood-handled steel rod laid across the top to exhibit that accessory cleaning tool. 45"H., 15½"TD., $275.00 – 295.00.

Butter Press/Worker/Roller

Ca. 1870–75. Pine; cast iron; splayed squared legs; marked REC'D PATENT; serrations on the metal lengths at each side mesh with handle-turned gears, causing the 1½"W., four oblong wood strips on a center roll to press out accumulated liquids left in the churned butter, those flowing out through an end hole into a bucket set beneath. This residue (usually) fed to the pigs. 19"H., 40½"L., $325.00 – 350.00.

Butter Press/Tray

Ca. early 1890s. Pine table on three legs; heavy squared-edge roller whose iron spear fit loosely through a rare "V" so it could be pulled back and forth; newly churned butter placed on the table was press-rolled until all excess liquids were drained out (buttermilk). 27"H., 39"DP., $325.00 – 350.00.

American forefathers could liberally use and savor the taste of homemade butter – piling it high on succulently dripping corn on the cob, mothers melted it for a croupy child, in cookery soaked it on cake/pastry tins or on brown paper used to line them; used it in doughs along with lard; combined it with horseradish, sometimes mint, for a variety of flavors.

Butter Workers

Butter hands. *Ca. early 1800s. Handcarved from one piece maple; fine grooves, regarded as better for making the tidbits. 10½"L., $38.00 pair.*

Butter scoop. *Ca. early 1800s. Handcarved from one piece maple; deep hook extension. 10¼"L., $135.00.*

Spade. *Ca. early 1800s. Handcarved from one piece maple; slight handle curve; different carving. 10¼"L., $50.00.*

Bucket
Ca. 1700s. One piece, slanted, handcarved from pine; set-in bottom; self-extended ears have a leather handle; carved Indian designs. 6"H., 5¾"TD., 6¼"BD., $225.00 – 250.00.

Butter Scoop/Indian Effigy Worker
Bird's head; from maple, 12½"L., $195.00.

Butter Hands/Rollers/ Scotch Hands

Ca. 1890s–1920s. Each one-piece maple medium-size grooves paddles and handles; used as a pair with butter between them for shaping butter balls and other fancy-shaped bits. 10"L., $42.50 each.

Butter Worker
Ca. 1800s. Maple; signed D.H. FOOT. 9¾"L., $75.00 – 95.00.

Butter Bowl and Butter Scoop/Worker
Ca. 1800s, handcarved. Bowl: handsome burl wood; 3¾"H., 3½"TD. Butter Scoop Worker (front center): maple, note the unusual edge of the scoop, almost as if rolled; 9"L., $325.00 set.

Butter Molds/Stamps (Prints)

Although known centuries B.C., butter was more widely used for lighting oils and medicinal ointments than for food. Decorating shaped blocks began in overseas kitchens, adopted by rural American homemakers. Each one chose a design, it was handcarved at home or by a craftsman, then area-restricted-to and separately-identified-as "her pattern." (Pewter and other metals followed.) To help earn needed extra monies, or when their animals gave more milk for drinking and resultant cream products than the cooks could use up and the family consume, excess printed molded butter was sold by the housewives at weekly "market stands," or from the backs of their buggies and wagons along the walkway in the nearest town. Today artifacts having fish, animals, birds, and oddities are foremost to collectors, but scarce – and expensive. (With the understanding the following are all BUTTER patterns, that word will not be repeated with each item; all are from the 1800s and from maple woods; exceptions noted.)

Swan Stamp
Diamond print circle, rushes; swan on the water; a small tight crack. 4½"D., $325.00.

Pinwheel Stamp
Ca. mid 1800s. Elaborately carved; note edge design. 4½"D., $310.00.

Letter and Lines Stamp
From a dark nutwood; lots of piecrust-edged lines; arcs, and an "H" with a big center dot. 3"H., 2½"D., $135.00.

Stars Stamp
Thick maple base with an oak handle; five smaller stars encircle a large deeply-carved center star; large edge scallops. 8½"H., $155.00.

Pewter Prints
Could be used for either butter or raw dough cookie press; four blocks can be divided; two plain and two lacy borders with a quiver of arrows, a leafy flower, a turkey on a hillock, and a peaked-roof house. $295.00.

Sheaves of Wheat Mold
Box-type dovetailed four corners; double pattern may be divided into an individual sheaf each; leaves; attractive dots borders. 3⅞"H., 6"W., $250.00.

Pennsylvania Dutch Oval Stamp

Ca. 1700s. The oldest print shown on these pages; hand-carved in walnut with a heart, daisy flower, stems and leaves, including a profuse usage of lines in a double row circle and center; underside handle is a squared corner oblong with a side split, no harm to its value. Design is characteristic of the Pennsylvania Germans. 2¾"H., 4"L., $325.00+.

Swan Stamp

Ca. mid 1800s. Graceful swan; tiny rickrack border; water; note carefully carved feathers and it even seems to have personality; reverse side knob handles. 2¾"D., $225.00.

Floral Stamp

Ca. 1700s. One of the oldest shown here; four prettily-petaled flowers on stems, a fern, leaves, and bordered concentric lines; reverse side knob handles. 3¾"D., $210.00.

Acorn Stamp

Deeply carved nut, stem, oak leaves, piecrust edge; reverse turned knob handle. 3¼"D., $195.00 – 225.00.

Lollipop Stamp

Ca. 1700s – early 1800s. To the maker's ideas, a five-petaled center dot flower; inverted mushroom knob completes end of handle; leaves. 7"H., 3½"D., $295.00.

Dove and Olive Branch Stamp

A fine carving but shallow and so age and soil darkened it is difficult to see its true worth; reverse short press handle. 2½"D., $195.00.

Fluted Flower Mold

Box type two-piece double designs, each piecrust border around a dot at each corner and a very deeply cut fluted-petaled flower in the center; stubby reverse side handle; box a bit "different" with wood bands rather than solid back. 8"L., 4½"W., $195.00.

Thistle Stamp

Prickly wildflower plus stem, leaves, and concentric lines; short reverse side handle. 4½"D., $145.00.

Flowers Stamp

Two four-petal each blossoms; big leaf; border lines; short reverse side handle. 3½"D., $125.00.

Sunflower Stamp

Sunflower and leaves pattern covers the whole stamp except for the border lines; short reverse side handle. 4¼"D., $195.00.

Box Mold

Ca. 1880. Pine; dovetailed four corners; extra-long press-down handle. 3⅝"H., 3¼"Square, $65.00.

Country Flowers Mold

Two four-petaled blooms on straight stem; leaves; circle-lines border. One-pound mold. 5½"H., 4½"D., $125.00 – 150.00.

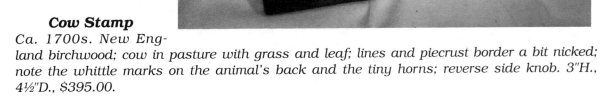

Tulip Mold
Popular motif with the Pennsylvania Dutch; mortised joints hold four pieces of wood together; center print can be lifted out of its (set-in) grooves for releasing molded-printed butter block and for cleaning. 7"H., 5"W., $395.00.

Cow Stamp
Ca. 1700s. New England birchwood; cow in pasture with grass and leaf; lines and piecrust border a bit nicked; note the whittle marks on the animal's back and the tiny horns; reverse side knob. 3"H., 4½"D., $395.00.

T.R. Hall Mold

Two pieces; cast aluminum; emb: T.R. HALL, 1 LB., BURLINGTON N.C.; wingnut type handle press that can go down through the open slot; four lines design. 4½"BD., $45.00.

Cow Stamp

Animal in field; portion of fence; leaf cluster; grasses; interesting two-border designs; attention given to detailing – as the cow's horns; reverse side knob handle. 3¾"D., $395.00.

Milk Can

Ca. early 1800s. Tinner made; larger cans were filled, left at the end of the lane to be picked up by the nearest dairy wagon; these smaller sizes were kept at home in cool, white-washed, walled "spring-houses" for the housewife to use for a family beverage, churning, making Schmear Kase (cottage cheese), and in creamed dishes, etc. Carried to market, she'd measure and ladle into jugs brought by customers. 9"H., 4⅛"BD., $75.00.

Milk Pail

Thin cobalt line on white gran-ite; the indenta-tion on each side near the top matches a small inside ledge on which the lid collar rests; lid turns to lock the pail and in reverse releases it; wire handle. 8"H., 6"TD., $45.00.

Milk Pail/Can

Ca. 1800s–1900s. Wood; wire handle swirled light and dark grays granite inside and out. 10½"H., 6½"D., $65.00.

Measuring Cup

Two-tone grays granite; wide pouring lip. 5½"H., 4"D., $25.00.

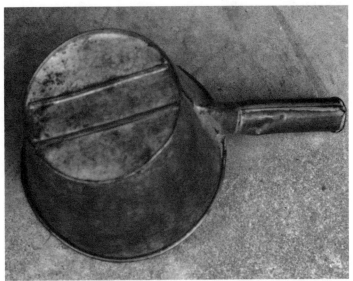

Milk Dipper

Ca. 1870. Gray tin, for milk or water; early wrapped seams; closed hollow handle. A ladle is a dipper, one commonly called the other, but long ago the utensil was first known as a ladle. 4¾"H., 8"TD., 5"L. handle, $45.00.

Milk Dipper

Ca. late 1800s. White, cobalt rimmed granite; to compensate for its heaviness when filled, there is an under-curve handle rest with top thumb grip. 6½"TD., $28.00.

Kitchen Milk Pitcher

Brass; maker advertisement: KREAMER, INC. With a "U.S." above this, could've originally been used in a military mess kitchen; soldered repairs on the handle and rim. 4½"H., $48.00.

Cream Dipper

Ca. late 1800s. Tinned cast iron; marked: YORK DAIRY, INC. 21"L. overall, bowl 5½"H., 5½"D., $95.00.

To pioneering Americans, from coastal Colonials to Settlers on remote outposts, water and food with its resultant cookery and wares (as has been since time began and ever will be) were by far their first considerations. Once those were established, their second need was clothing for their families. And so, gradually, fields began to grow and expand and flocks and herds began to multiply.

Cotton field near Rome, Georgia, with some bolls bursting open, several in pods; a shrubby plant, seeds in capsules, three wide-lobed leaves; a vegetable fiber providing staple clothing.

Meat for the kitchens, wool for clothing and more . . .

Northwestern New York State sheep, curious about our presence, didn't (couldn't) realize his impact on human progression; that fine wool stretches one-third of its length. By 200 B.C., Romans had begun to improve their flocks; American Settlers were forced into raising sheep by English import tariffs. And beyond their wool, they gave to our frontiers mutton and lamb when food was so vital. 'Tis said the busiest people can always find time to do one more thing . . . well, pioneer wives after first feeding their families, and finishing the endless daily chores . . . still welcomed the additional tasks of raising their own crops and flocks, keeping their looms close at hand in the kitchen to sit down "every whipstitch," weaving a little between looking into pots and pans steaming on the hearth and checking browning bread, among other things.

Wool Comb

Ca. 1700s. Turned wood handles; smithy forged square nails; combs are the iron wire that penetrate the wooden sides. 12"L., 4"W. bases, $165.00.

Yarn Winder

Ca. latter 1800s. Handturned maple; three wide splayed legs; can be set for turns needed; incomplete. 28"D. wheel, $225.00+.

Yarn Winder

Ca. early 1800s. All original; turning the round metal dowel-like iron rod that goes through the center squared wood length, fastened to the opposite upright, activates the device. 31"H., $225.00 – 250.00+.

Yard Winder

Ca. 1850. All mortised construction, handmade from heart pine; note crutch-like ends of yard winders. 22½"L., base 19"L., 11"W., $225.00.

Yarn Winder

Ca. 1800. Clock/Clack Reel/Handwinder – names familiar in different areas. Maple; all original; has a simple gear-meshing clacker; winds thread to be spun; moved out of the way when not in usage – as a corner – in cold weather it was moved in usage close to fireside, when the yarn was spun, it was replaced by the spinning wheel; set at a required number of revolutions (customarily 40); when the hand turned wheel at the back reached that point, a wood clapper meshed with a gear, loudly clacking finish of that skein. 40"H., 21"F. wheel, $275.00+.

Spills Frame

Ca. 1850s. Tennessee dealer calls it "slicks"; Ohio origin; heavy gauge black iron spikes (spills) hold (for display only) 12 yarn-wrapped bobbins. Overall with frame 13"L., 10"W., $55.00 – 75.00.

Darning Eggs

Black japanned wood; designed handle; made in two pieces. 6¼"L., $25.00.

Carved from one piece of maple inlaid with darker ovals; uncommon. 6"L., $35.00.

Flax Spinning Wheel

Ca. 1840. Dark stained. 39"H., 40"L., 25½"D. wheel, $525.00+.

Flax Spinning Wheel

Maple; flax wheels were easier to carry and store than the larger heavier wool wheels; not so many of the latter seen now in shops. Many French Canadians of the Quebec regions painted their wheels, some have been refinished to the natural wood – look for color remaining in wood pores. Flax fibers, obtained from an annual herb genus plant was woven 3,500 years ago as linen by Egyptians – a cloth symbol of purity cloaking their priests, and others of Greek and Jewish faiths. It was an adaptable fiber, able to be coarsely woven as in sailcloth or finely woven into filmy garments. 26¼"H., 20"L., 6"W., $425.00 – 450.00+.

----◆----

Coverlet

Navy and white; two parts sewn together (made on small narrow loom). Nearing the end of marking her warm heavy coverlet, patterned in American eagles, smaller birds, roses, trees, and starpoint designs inside a cross-diamonds border, Jane M. Collins included her name, homeplace of Newfane, Niagara County, N.Y., and the year 1858. Ever carefully cherished, present day owners in a nearby village on Lake Ontario occasionally drape this (mint condition) artifact over a settle's back, just as for almost 150 years it must have been put out on another fireside kitchen bench when folks stopped by. 6' x 7½', $695.00+.

Coverlets and related "throws" were sometimes made by itinerant weavers going from home to home. Bringing his own small loom, weaving for anyone able to hire him, upon request he'd add the buyer's name, etc., then he'd move on to another homestead or village.

----◆----

Kitchen Living

While homes were expanding through the years, the following pieces may have been moved into extended spaces, many remaining in the kitchens, most are still regarded under the classification of "country" or "kitchen furniture." And so, with that definition established, the word "kitchen" will not preface the name of every object.

Slat-back Chair

Ca. 1850. Painted mixed woods; original cowhide seat; also handy as a churning chair; two top slats when made matched the lowest; one upright split. Green Cove Springs Museum. N.P.A.

Slat-back Side Chair

Ca. 1840–50. All original Shaker style in maple; typical finials; upcurved slats; rounded posts; splint seat. $195.00 – 225.00.

Arrow-back Side Chair

Ca. 1860. Pine and maple; rolled front planked seat; one shaped stretcher; three splayed legs – one at front unlike the others so it evidently is a repair replacement. 31"H., 15"DP seat, $275.00 – 295.00.

Rod-back Armchair

Ca. 1875. Pine with maple plank seat; low stretchers; out-curved head rest; heavy arms with Pennsylvania style curled-under hand rests; narrowly base-tapered legs. $265.00.

Slat-back Rocking Chair

Ca. 1860–70. All original; flattened uprights ending in donkey/mule/rabbit ear tops; rockers socketed to legs – sometimes with low stretchers, the rockers have been added to a straight chair; note uncommon button-shaped turnings between lower and upper side uprights – such seat and back joinings a typically Southern style; and as the dealer said "good for another hundred years." 30½"H., top slat 4"W., $175.00.

Rocking Chair

Ca. mid 1800s. Moravian hand fashioned; tiger maple and hickory; unusual stiles; thin armrests tapered at the back and held by slanted posts that fit into the top thickest stretcher on each underside of the chair; legs socketed into rockers; restored seat woven to the original. 43⅞"H., $255.00.

Moravians immigrated into this country, settling in Pennsylvania and North Carolina after 1735. From there they branched out into other states.

Rocker

Ca. late 1700s. Comb-back Windsor; has the typical mixed woods and uneven number of spindles; saddle seat; splayed legs socketed into rockers. 43½"H., 18½"W., 17½"DP. seat, $895.00+.

Slat-back Rocker

Ca. 1840–50. Hand fashioned maple; narrow squared arms dip at center and taper where joined into uprights; type of spool finials noted on similar early 1800s Ohio chairs; seat is newly woven rushes. 43¾"H. seat 12" from floor, 21"W. at front, 15"W. at back, $695.00+.

Rocking chairs were a common sight at fireside in the 18th and early 19th centuries where living was all – or principally – in the kitchens.

Side Chair

Ca. 1850–60. New England factory-made in birch and maple; rolled front of shaped plank seat; wide headrest; Pennsylvania style turned spindles only as high as middle slat. 33"H., 17" from floor; 15½"W. front, $450.00 variable to area.

Youth Chair

Ca. 1850. Hand fashioned; all original except newly woven splint seat; mixed woods; cannonball finials; splayed two front legs; interestingly shaped armrests; stretchers go into the posts, typical of most 19th century chairs. 32½"H., 12"W. seat front, $175.00+.

Cupboard

Ca. 1900. Pine; handsomely grooved cornice (cornices regarded as denoting fine workmanship); tongue and groove joinings; four shelves; iron concealed hinges expertly installed; spring door latches with polished iron knobs; handy stepback ledge. 54½"H., 23"W., $475.00.

Closed Cupboard

Ca. 1860–70. North Georgia origin; pine; all original; sides, base, doors, and three inside shelves are each of one-board construction; whittled turn latches above might have been added later; glass knobs; stepback ledge mighty handy. 74"H., 11"DP. stepback, $1,300.00.

Document Box

Ca. 1700s. Leather-covered wood; lavishly decorated with brass studs that also practically held strips; solid brass chased pull on key keeper – original key missing (but one can be duplicated); naturally age-darkened wood interior (might even be a bit discolored from holding deeds, etc. printed in the more destructible early inks); in early one-room cookery/living dwellings, boxes of this type, vastly important, were often stashed under a bed in a far corner or set in the loft. 6½"H., 9½"L., 6"W., $250.00 – 300.00.

Blanket Chest

Ca. 1840. Original green paint on six-board pine; dovetailed four corners; iron catch added later when first one may have been broken; two riveted-on iron patches hold together the top that has split under heavy usage (probably from being hauled in a covered wagon); rodent gnawings; still holding on after rough times. 19¼"H., 39"W., 17"DP., $275.00.

Trunk

Ca. early 1800s. Pine; New England origin; black recently painted iron fixtures; once a tray rested inside on the side rails; was used for "small clothes" before the family had a proper cabinet, and wood pegs or nails driven into the walls were overloaded with heavy outer clothing; these flat-top trunks are now in demand for low practical coffee or chairside tables. 13"H., 17"W., 30"L., $150.00.

Footwarmer

Ca. late 1700s. Rarely seen in walnut; hand fashioned; wire bail and box for hot coals; decoratively pierced; no-harm rodent hole in front corner; front panel slides up and lifts off. 6½"h., 9½"W., 8"DP., $395.00+.

These footwarmers warmed cold feet when they were beside or briefly on top; kept close at fireside to comfort when chilling drafts swept across the floor – to enjoy on limited rest periods between getting together meals and other kitchen chores – and when dusk fell and the housewife could take a deep breath until the morrow; carried in wagons and later "rigs" (carriages) to church and other "gatherings"; it was an essential if the mister could make one or afford to order it from the settlement craftsman.

Footwarmer

Ca. late 1800s. All original, hand fashioned from rare tiger and birdseye maple; wire bail; crookedly placed bored holes; dovetailed corners; heavy gauge tin box inside for coals; front slides up and lifts off. 6½"H., 9½"W., 8"DP., $375.00+.

---◆---

Footwarmer

Ca. early 1800s. All original, homemade from native pine; tin liner; leather strap carrier; sliding door for inserting a natural stone chipped to proper size and shape, first thoroughly warmed down hearth (later on bricks could be used heated the same way or in an oven if one was available); heat emission holes intended to be bored in a straight line for appearance as well; upper New York State origin along Lake Ontario. 7½"H., 9"W., 3¼"DP., $225.00.

---◆---

---◆---

Drysink

Ca. 1700s. Pennsylvania homemade from local pine; faded red paint unable to disguise traces of even earlier white; one inside shelf; one-board door on iron hinges; whittled turn latch; if there was ever a bottom board it is now gone; however, the dealer believes it was the maker's intention to make it, but in a one-room dwelling with so many chores he simply hadn't time to finish the furniture – and his wife needed it. Several rodent holes in rear base boards. 33"H., 38½"W., 19¾"DP., $465.00.

---◆---

Drysink

Ca. 1700s. Pennsylvania pine from one-piece boards; stripped of original white paint, bits still cling; two inside shelves; smithy-forged square head nails, iron fixtures; curved bracket feet are extensions of 18¾"W. board sides. (Those handles sticking up are on baskets sittng on top of drysink.) $525.00+.

Used today as for over 200 years – for storage of utensils – but without the other earlier daily washing up of table and cooking items in a dishpan set down in the trough. Drysinks, important to housewives in kitchens past,

were factory produced in quantities in the 1820s to 1830s. Presently, they reside in any room, but with emphasis, of course, where they have always primarily belonged – in cooking areas.

Drysink

Ca. 1800s. Found by a dealer in a Tennessee barn; homemade from pine "on the place"; maker's initials "HBH" cut into door's inside crossbar; butterfly hinges are new; smithy made nails; white paint was stripped but still apparent in wood pores; note wood-wrapped corners; whittled turn latch on one-piece door; two inside shelves are each 16½"DP; splashboard at sides and top back is 4"H.; maker used random boards in the back (which means he used whatever wood was left on hand since they were to be at the back – a common practice on old furniture.) 32"H., 25½"W., $495.00+.

Dough Raiser Table

Early; rare style; hand fashioned poplar is the primary wood along with tiger maple; breadboard ends (these to keep boards from warping); two-board wide lift-off lid/table top, one board 17½"W, the other 16"W, both 50"L. The top can be lifted off to reveal a large doughraiser space inside; ball knobs touch the floor at the base of turned tapered legs. (On many of these dough raisers, bread could be kneaded on the board top). 30"H., 50"W., $1,475.00.

Dough Box/Raiser

Ca. mid 1800s. Mennonite origin; pine; all original; two long handholds in-curved for gripping were to lift separate lids. 29½"H., 31"L., 16"DP., $450.00 – 495.00.

Mennonites are a Christian sect devoted to plainness of dress and material things, who pioneered as among the first Europeans to William Penn's colony.

Ice Box

Ca. 1900s. Pine; iron fixtures; zinc coated heavy tin liner; tongue and groove sides; lift-top covers a wood shelf slatted for an ice block's melting to run off into a drainage hole in the bottom half; lower inside shelf; these are heavily reproduced. 48"H., 28"W., 22"DP., $325.00 – 350.00.

Meal (Cornmeal) Bin

Ca. 1800s. Chestnut; two inner compartments; iron nails and hinges; underside of lid painted white and traces indicate it may have been so overall; front is one-board wide, 17" and 1" thick wood; turned knob-top legs are tapered extensions of curved around corners almost to the top of the bin; uncommon workmanship. 34½"W., 20"DP., $450.00 – 495.00.

Pie Safe

Ca. 1860s. A local piece handmade at Cave Spring, Georgia during the Civil War period, 1861-1865. All original, entirely wood pinned; four inside shelves (now used for linen storage); stained red with oxen's blood as the basic ingredient – not an uncommon practice in furniture staining 100 or more years ago, particularly in rural regions; punched from the inside out and wood framed – the quality type of workmanship on these safes. Four center tin panels have pinwheel type six-point stars and their four corners are circular dot designs; two top and two bottom tins have various dot patterns – all to the maker's own ideas. Each one-board side continues to form two short feet; hinged doors have wood pullouts, one also with a whittled turn-latch; key is missing; shaped gallery at one side has a fairly large stain (only removable by finishing the whole gallery), this from long-vanished mud daubers (wasps or mud wasps) which, to many collectors proves interesting. 65"H., 53"W., 20"DP., $1,000.00 – 1,200.00.

Pie Safe

Ca. early 1800s. Homecrafted "on the place" from heart pine (meaning from the heart of a pine tree, fine grained wood from the yellow pine, straight and comparatively knot-free from the white pine, terms heard mostly in Virginia and further south); original green paint; black fine mesh screening reveals two inside shelves; wide whittled latch – the iron pull probably added later – rodent hole (which entries are sometimes faked but not too successfully); original gnawings on early artifacts, generally speaking as to values, unless personally offensive to a buyer, should be kept "as is" – if not too unsightly. 46"H., 38¾"W., 21"DP., $995.00 – 1,200.00.

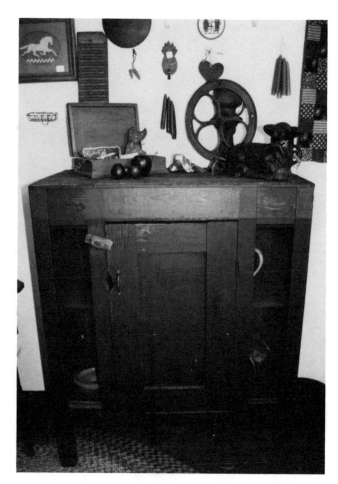

Pie Safe

Ca. early 1800s. All original; still struggling to retain some if its blue paint; a long tin repair patch at one topside corner may be covering a large rodent gnawing or the wood could've been splintered moving the furniture piece about; six wood-framed tin panels punched in the quality way – from the outside in – each has a large center star design surrounded by patterned dots; three inside shelves; whittled turn latch at the top but a hole halfway down one door panel indicates another closure may have been there; legs are square tapered, extensions of the side boards, stains indicating they may have stood at times in small tins of water to ward off ants. 53"H., 36"W., 13"DP top overhang, 14"DP., $1,250.00 – 1,500.00.

Fireside Stool/Cricket

Ca. early 1800s. Handmade; black painted; one-piece curved sides end in bracket feet; the sides mortised through the seat are slashed and wood-pegged at center in the old way of strengthening stools; under-color of white shows in nicks. $225.00 – 250.00.

Fireside Stool

Ca. 1700s. Farm homemade from one of its own hickory trees; one side of the 2" thick seat was cut or has been worn thinner; four legs are irregularly splayed; kept close at fireside as stool, footrest, or even taken outside for milking and other sit-down chores. 11"H. one side, 9"H. the other, 12"L., 9½"W., $125.00+.

Hearthside Stool

Ca. 1870. Shaker; signed; on the bottom as the Shaker trademark in red at center: "Rocking Chair with SHAKERS', Mt. Lebanon, N.Y."; original dark stain; plank top; deep apron, and center bulged and ringed legs that taper at the floor. 7"H., 5½"W., $525.00+.

Work Table

Ca. 1880s. Oak base, two-board pine top; tapered legs; self knob on drawer that with patience will close properly. 29½"H., 30"W., 24½"DP., $295.00.

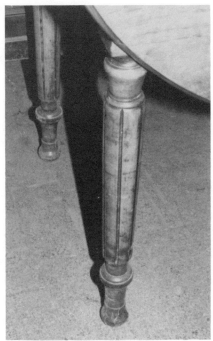

Eating Table

Ca. 1870. Chestnut; dealer tagged: "From an old kitchen in rural Florida"; rounded ends, the drop sides convenient to wall placement; designed legs are eloquent of "shoes banging against," easily rubbed and polished out. 29"H., 42½"L., 24½"W., $425.00 – 450.00.

Candle Molds

Ca. 1800s. Tin; these, patterned after an early simple style, long iron tubes with strap handles and set in bases, gradually developed from a mold process thought to have begun in Paris during the 1400s. With scarcity of tinsmiths' raw materials in

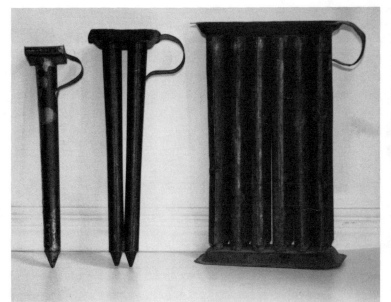

the Colonies, candle-making for lighting and ceremonies by the long tedious task of dipping necessarily continued. In the mid 1700s, however, rolling mills began to produce, and many housewives were able to pour wax in six to 24 molds. After petroleum and its products made possible the common usage of oil lamps, candle molds were no longer vital. Today, the one- and two-section molds are rare and usually more expensive. One tube, 10¼"H., soldered repairs, $195.00 – 225.00; two tube, 10¾"H., $225.00 – 235.00; four tube, 11"H., $225.00 – 275.00; 12 tube, 11½"H., $200.00 – 225.00.

Candle Mold

Ca. 1800s. Maple; 24 pewter candle tubes; floor style not plentiful today; ends are each one board wide ending in bracket feet; this seen in upper New York state. 17½"H., 21"L., 7½"W., $1,300.00+.

Candle Holder

Ca. 1700s. A rarity to find; hand fashioned in hickory and pine; double sockets; ratchet control for lifting to 28"–30" high; a simple wood-whittled holding bar fastened to one upright side falls into the proper notch in the sawtooth center riser, then in reverse ratchet action, the candle can be lowered by the same method. (New candles for display). 14"H., 9½"W., base 3½"DP., $300.00 – 325.00.

Candle Box

Ca. mid 1800s. Pine with finger notch in its sliding chamfered top lid; hand fashioned in New England. 10"H., 6"W., 5"DP., $185.00 – 195.00.

Improved Spiral Candle Holder

Ca. 1700s. A rarity; iron wire; this improved model stemmed from rush lights poorer Europeans used, carried over here and used along with other devices by the Pilgrims. The corkscrew "helix" is an ingenious "elevator" that keeps the candle raised as it burns. Collectors may unwittingly pass it up should one ever appear, for it little expresses at a glance its vast heritage significance in lighting. 6⅞"H., 4½"D., $245.00+.

Whether a chamberstick, candle holder, or candelabrum and such called by these and other names, they all support the wick-centered wax burners. Oldest among them is the Pricket Stick which impales a candle on its long spear-like point, a type noted among many church holders.

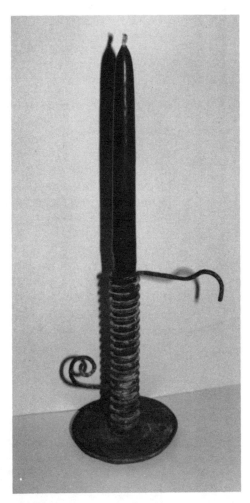

Hogscraper Candlestick

Ca. early to mid 1800s. Black sheet iron; top spur was hangup on a chair seat or back; with the stem as a handle, at fall butchering time the bristles of a prepared hog were scraped off, the pedestal the tool; original pushup works. 7½"H., 4¼"D., $125.00.

Candlestick

Ca. 1820. Brass, saucer base; workable pushup as original. 3½"H., 4½"BD., $110.00.

Low Candle Holder

Ca. 1800s. Tinner made; set on the eating table where it could extend the flickering fireplace light so the wife perhaps could sew and the husband could read to the children or hear their lessons. 5"D., $55.00.

Primitive Oil Lamp

Ca. early 1700s. Tinner made – may be from left-over odds and ends – reflector; uncommonly shaped wick pick held with a leather strip; could sit flat or be hung in cracks in the walls or in the mortar between the logs; sooty and black from years of giving a feeble but determined smoky illumination.

Wick picks cleaned cloth burners and were the stick picks for hanging; a cloth laid in the bowl, one end in tallow and animal oils, etc. – never pig nor fish if humanly possible to prevent it – that filled the cup burned at the other end laid in the protruding groove. Lamps were hung as close as possible to the fireplaces so that drafts might carry the offensive odors (and smoke) up and out the chimneys. Whale oil was more than welcomed when it became available. $195.00 – 225.00.

Grease Lamps
Ca. early 1800s. A single bowl ($175.00) and two nesting ($145.00); in hand forged iron; Betty Lamp bowls; twisted wire picks.

Lamp Holder
Ca. 1800s. Wrought iron; fashioned to look like a snake. N.P.A.

Chamberstick
Ca. 1880. Black japanned tin; looped strap handle. 2¼"H., 5½"D., $48.00.

Finger Lamp
Tin, brass, soldered seams; original wick; dated 1890; new glass chimney; burned kerosene. $65.00.

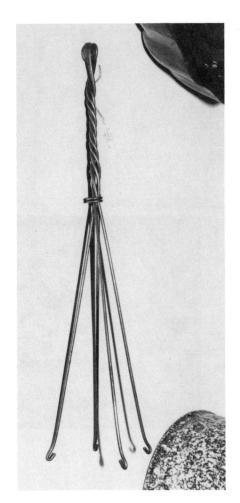

Lamp Cleaning Rods

Ca. 1800s. Blackened iron; twisted at tops to form handle; can move rods about on a spring action; cotton or bits of cloth attached to hooks gathered the soot and dirt off chimneys and from inside lamp bases. 13"L., $25.00.

Wick Trimmer

Ca. 1860. Scissors-shaped metal; sharp inside straight edge snipped burned wick ends of candles and oil lamps against the sharp edge of the other part, charred threads falling into the cup. 5½"H., $65.00.

Finger Lamp

Ca. 1800s. Tin, brass, glass chimney, several no-harm small dents; emb: STERLING. 7½"H., $75.00 – 85.00.

Oil Lamp

Ca. 1820. A form rarely seen today; of Flemish origin; brass; was rarely made in copper; the wick lies in the upper spout with the lower spout to catch any oil overflow. (Neat and frugal as the oil could be re-used). 14"H., $250.00 – 275.00.

Match Holder

Ca. 1890. Ironstone; probably originally held long sulphur-tipped wooden matches; outside is slanted and grooved for striking surfaces. 2⅜"H., 1⅞"TD., 2¾"BD., $65.00.

Kerosene Can

Ca. 1900s. Marked THE DANDY; tin, wood, wire; screw top gone; the glass inside the metal case, with windows to check kerosene level during usage; a beautiful aqua blue. Used to fill reservoirs of all manner of household lamps. $38.00.

Lamp Filler

Ca. 1800s. Tinner made to hold whale oil for filling illuminating devices. Fancy small hinged triangle is the lid hinge. (One dealer noted that reproductions are presently copying this old model in tins for imported olive oils.) 10"H., 4½"BD., $55.00.

Charcoal Irons

Bearded Man. *Ca. 1800s. Pat. marked 1852; cast iron; wood handles; large heat vent; hinged lift lid to fill; sliding panel; emb: "W.D. Cummings & E. Bless." 9¾"H., $225.00.*
Lion's Head. *Ca. 1800s. Cast iron; wood handles; scalloped edge on hinged lip top which iron head locks after iron is filled to use. 9"H., $225.00.*

Primer

Brass, wood pressure bar knob. 7"L.

Gas Iron

Ca. 1910. Coleman Instant Lite Iron; nickel plated iron; shaped wood handle painted green; black knob. 11"L.

$138.00 set.

Trivet

Ca. 1700s. Handwrought iron; wood-shaped handle with brass ferrule; three feet with carefully curled (scrolls) ends; shape customarily intended for pressing irons. 11¼"L., $165.00.

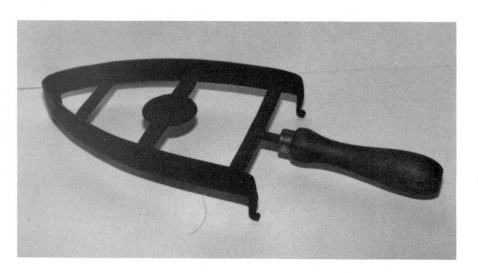

Graniteware

Pieces combined by a dealer as a set; white and cobalt; these all might have been kept on a bucket-type bench near the back (kitchen) door for a quick dousing upon getting up mornings, after work in the fields, or for the cook freshening up before setting out a meal. Pitcher, 10"H., 6"TD.; basin, 4"H., 13½"TD.; dipper, 13¼"L., 2½"TD.; cup, 1¾"H., 2¾"TD., $65.00 set.

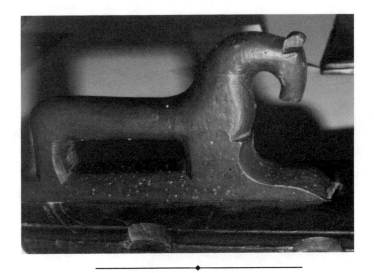

Smoothing Board

Ca. 1830 or earlier. When the family moved up from corn shucks mattresses into those stuffed with saved feathers, one more chore for the cook was to smooth down the pads every morning (if there were young girls in the household the job was relegated to them); probably carried here by Scandinavian immigrants; handcrafted; original paints in red, green, and black in subdued tones; armored head resembles that of a Viking; note the antler-like horns with leaves, the necklace a man usually wore; the high collar and ruffle at neckline. A full carved animal in the handgrip. RARE. 22"L., 6"W., $495.00 – 525.00.

Wash Boiler

All original; black and green painted on copper – lid missing; labeled: PENN METAL WARE CO. WILKES BARRE, PA. 13"H., 11"W., $125.00 – 135.00.

Scrub Pail

Ca. 1900s. Galvanized tin; wood; soldering repairs; no holes. 5½"H., 11½"TD., $20.00.

Wash Stick

Ca. 1800s. Handcarved hickory in New England; prongs soap stained; used to move about and lift out clothes soaked or washed in a tub; one shorter side indicates the housewife habitually leaned harder on that prong. One prong, 15"L.; the other, 14¾"L., $38.00.

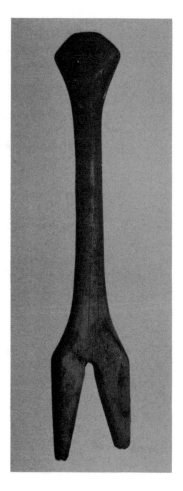

Wash Board

Ca. 1800s–1900s. Bentwood, galvanized tin; ledge at bottom of age and usage split top arch with its metal to resist dampness of water and the soap caustics; large ridges for scrubbing rough garments. 23"H., 12¾"W., $48.00.

Dish Pan

Ca. 1800s. A different pattern in gray granite. 6"H., 14¼"TD., $38.00.

Wash Board

Ca. 1800s–1900s. Pine frame; galvanized tin ridges for lighter-weight clothes; printed: THE UNIVERSAL TOP NOTCH SOAP SAVING; Sanitary Front Drain – this broken drain is a bit uncommon. National Wash Board Co., Chicago, Ill. 26½"H., 14"W., $68.00.

Soap Saver/Swisher/Shaker

Heavy gauge wire; wood; first patented about 1875, continuing into the 1900s; opens on a hinge; frugally made possible using small pieces left over from original large bars of soap. 10½"L., $14.00.

Wash Pan

Ca. 1890s. Gray and white granite. 2⅜"H., 12"TD., $38.00.

Leftovers

Whatever isn't consumed at a meal is a leftover. Even had they been magicians of preparation, cooks couldn't (can't) always serve the exact amount of food that will be eaten. Long ago, without our refrigeration advantages, more-perishable dishes remaining from the "big" noon dinner were carried out to a cool "springhouse" or cellar, while jellies, pastries, and the like were left right on the table, lightly cloth covered. (Everyone then didn't much care for leftovers – any more than some do now – but on the table they went, a start for supper). The items featured here, while not leftovers in the sense of food, did contribute to the general well-being of families. Unable to fit tidily into a special grouping among these pages, still may you further enjoy "looking at" these things from kitchens past.

Coconut Tin

SNOWDRIFT BRAND SWEETENED FANCY SHRED COCONUT, SPECIAL PREPARED WITH SUGAR, GLYCERIN, & SALT, FRANKLIN BAKER COMPANY, N.Y.; original red, white, and black paper label; wire handles; tight lid. 13¾"H., 12¼"D., $75.00 – 95.00.

Because of their charm and practicality, many of these metal and wood containers are sought by collectors to decorate today's kitchens and entertainment rooms. Their bright, easy designs make for perfect conversational "ice breakers."

Tea Bin

All original black japanned tin; white, gold, red, and green designs; painted: E. BREAKFAST. 28"H., 22"W., $175.00.

Washing Soda Box

All original paper-covered bentwood; wire cleats fasten wrapped oak bands; black, white, yellow label: MONROE TAYLOR'S GRANULATED WASHING SODA NO. 113 WATER ST., NEW YORK; in circled chief's head in feathered regalia: GOLD MEDAL IS THE BEST; held 112 lbs. of soda; heavy blue paper lined; lift knob depressed; first from village general store, this was found in a 1900s rural kitchen; paper label recommends that when empty, it can be kept on a shelf for sugar or on the floor for flour, and warns the user to keep box away from dampness. 16"H., 14"TD., $75.00.

Horse Doorstop

Ca. 1890s. Cast iron; complete with reins and saddle; elaborately detailed pedestal. This stood at the kitchen door near the fireplace and seemingly became covered with dust from the ashes. 9½"H., 8½"L. nose to tail. $175.00.

Doorstops or door porters have been made in some quantities from the 1790s, sometimes found with an upright rod for easier handling. This held the door open wide into the steamy kitchen, desired to get more air to ease the perspiring cook as she prepared the big noonday meal. When a home gained more rooms-status, door porters were still used in kitchens as well as in dining rooms and parlors for also letting in more light.

Doorstop

Ca. 1800s. Cat with a Bow; half animal cast in iron; marked Hubley; post-civil War; nicely detailed – note cat's expression. $125.00.

Doorstop

Scottish Terrier, *cast iron, two sides cast separately and then joined; painted black; cute pose. 8"H., 11"L., $135.00.*

Witches' Balls

Ca. 1700s–1800s. "Handed down" from many generations, blown glass balls in pale and deep green; filled with common table salt, they were hung beside the fireplace to keep salt dry – and handy for the cook. Folklore has it that if a witch came down the chimney and saw its reflection in the glass, the witch scatted back up the chimney in a hurry! Another family's version of this tale is that positively wiping off soot gathered on the balls exorcised ghostly intruders. Another housewife said her forebears hung them at the kitchen window to ward off bad luck and evil doings. 5"H. and 3¼"H., $45.00 each.

Lock & Key

Ca. 1895. Cast iron; removed right off the kitchen door at the estate sale of an abandoned early home once thriving on the banks of north Florida's St. John's River; thumb latch in working condition. 5½"H., 4¾"W. Rarely available original key. 4¾"L., $75.00.

Road Sign

Ca. 1900 and continuing in some rural areas. Farmer's wife hung this sign at the end of a dirt lane on a field fence fronting an Indiana county road; red, black, and white painted; when there was a surplus of eggs beyond her own cooking needs, she tacked a paper – or wrote in chalk – in the black square provided, indicating eggs for sale that day and the price. If the space was blank or cloth covered, no eggs were available. Welcome extra coins for her cash box, she usually "sold out" to built-up regular customers who drove out from the nearby town in their wagons and "rigs." When automobiles became generally more affordable, her business grew even more rapidly, townsfolk wanting fresh country eggs. They carried their own baskets and the wife carefully paper-wrapped each egg before packing. Steady customers were often invited into the farmhouse kitchen for a cooling glass of buttermilk. 11½"H., 20½"L., $95.00.

Hot Water Cans

Ca. 1800's. Set of three hand fashioned copper; ring arcs to lift center hinged lid half; comfortable holder on handle; good pouring length spouts. 17"H., 12"H., 10"H., $600.00.

Water Can

Galvanized tin, wire, wood; inverted acorn white porcelain finial on lid; hinged spout cover opens for pouring; closed it protects from dirt and insects; tilt bar. 16"H., $58.00.

Tidy Rack/Comb Case

Ca. early 1900s. Several times painted tin; few mold spots on original mirror; usually hung at the back kitchen door for a quick brushup before going out. 11½"H., 8¾"W., $32.50.

Soap Dish

White painted tin; scalloped edges, stamped designs. 6"W., 3¼"DP., $32.50.

Grocer's Christmas Plate

White porcelain, gilt letters. ¼" border, 7¼"D., $145.00.

Grocers sometimes gave a Christmas bonus (or a small brown paper sack of hard candies) to customers keeping weekly charge slips current.

More and more manufacturers and wholesalers inserted a (premium) kitchenware item or recipe book into food stuffs packages to introduce and promote sales. Often their wares were sent out in cotton bags which, when emptied, could be converted into aprons and even children's clothing. (Great now for those same type aprons, kitchen-country look in curtains and settle pillows.)

Moxie Server

Pressed glass with raised lettering; the company organized in 1884 selling their "nerve tonic to make you feel better"; in the 1930s, with successful marketing, they entered the field of soft drinks. 3¼"H., 2¼"D., $68.00.

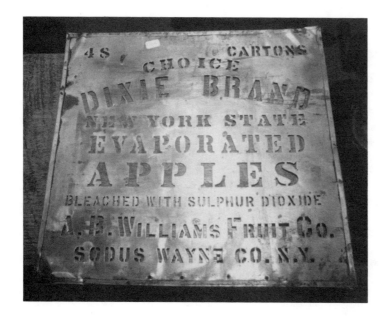

Stencil

Copper; for marking boxes of fruit shipped from A.B. Williams Fruit Co. $95.00 – 125.00.

With better shipping advantages liberally stocking stores, and home gardens providing more than families could themselves eat, advertising was bound to emerge . . . announcements publicizing sales of commodities. (Ancient Egyptians proclaimed arrivals of ships' cargoes via town criers.) The invention of printing grew into innumerable types of enticements, as men walking city streets, for one, carrying heavy wooden shoulder-fastened front and back "sandwich boards" offering menus of restaurants . . . all evolving into today's sophisticated versions . . . but food has always been predominant.

Preservation of foods has ever been of main concern to humans . . . since indefinite antiquity when the sun's rays and open fires were used for drying meats, fish, nuts, berries, grains, fruits, etc. Later Scottish wives parched meal from oats as our Indians treated corn. (Dried corn puddings and schnitz, dried apple pies, were requested settlement potluck treats). Pemmican, an American Indian staple for winter tepee storage and convenient in moving about, was hot melted animal fats or oils poured over finely-pounded meats mixed with dried berries and the like, formed into cakes next packed into animal skin bags . . . pemmican historically declared quite "palatable."

Framed Rice Advertisement Card

Ca. 1901. Cook's Flaked Rice; note sun rising at center. $35.00.

Colman's Mustard Box

Only Gold Medal Paris 1878; By Special Warrant to the Queen; Bull's Head Trademark. 4"H., 20½"W., 12"DP., $145.00.

Cream Corn Starch Box

Dovetailed four corners; "Scientifically Pre-pared Expressly for Food." $75.00.

Stoneware Bowl

Very old; family-used for cornstarch puddings and such. 2½"H., 8"D., $68.00.

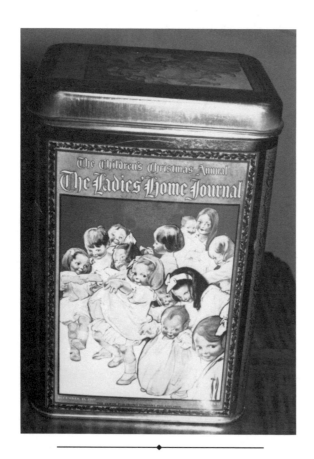

Biscuit/Cookie Tin

December 15, 1910, "The Ladies' Home Journal." $125.00.

Borden's Malted Milk Tin

Ca. 1910. Meadow Brand; red and white; found in Virginia. 9½"H., 5¼"Square, $35.00.

Grape Nuts Tin

14 oz.; yellow and black; signed "C.W. Post, Factory Always Open To Visitors." Postum Cereal Company, Battle Creek, Mich., U.S.A. $28.00.

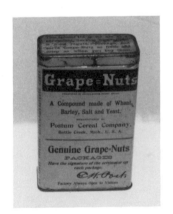

Tins

Snow King Baking Powder. *$38.00.*
Princine. *Patented Nov. 23, 1915. Original contents; the empty tin becomes a handled measuring and drinking cup. $78.00.*
Ontario Peanut Butter Pail. *With wire bail. $45.00.*

Coronation Tea Tin 1911

English; bright lithographs in blue, red, white, yellow, green, and gilt. Double freshness is insured by inside fine wire ring lift lid. 7¼"H., 9¼"W., 5¾"DP., $345.00.

Such bright items were important to manufacturers, especially those in uncommon shapes and/or depicting heritage events. Original tins have been heavily reproduced, but enough old ones survive to warrant seeking.

McLaughlin's XXXX Roasted Coffee Card

Children and kittens; "Attention is called to the continued success and satisfaction given by McLaughlin's." $28.00.

Egg Carrier

"STAR EGG CARRIER AND TRAYS MFG. CO., Rochester, N.Y. Pat. Mar. 10, '03; Can. Dec. 19, '05; Eng. Apr. 14, '05"; other patents pending; mortised corners wood box with iron wire handle with folding paper individual spaced for security. 6½"W., 8¼"L., $78.00.

Pine Framed Sign

Ca. 1920. DEKALB "Profit Pullets." (Pullets are young hens not yet a year old.) $225.00.

Detecto Store Scale

Used in a store, then at a farmer's market stand, and also at a mill for weighing small purchases. 16"H., 18"W., $145.00.

Cream Can

For dairy farm's pickup; brass plate imp: ELKIN'S DAIRY; holds 4 qts. of cream. 10"H., 7"BD., $78.00.

Dairy Farm Tin Sign

BAILAND FARMS; framed; white, black and green. 23¾"H., 36"W., $275.00 – 295.00.

Milk Pitcher

Used on a farm kitchen table about 1861. Old Hall earthenware from Mother Hubbard series; fruit and leaf bands along with child blowing bubbles; rarity; a lip crack was professionally repaired – now difficult to detect. 7¾"H., 3¾"TD., 4¼"BD., $425.00 – 450.00.

Jelly Mold

Tin; very old. 6"D., 3"DP., $55.00.

Spring Cake Pan

Center can be lifted out; one side clamped, $45.00.

Can Opener

Ca. 1900. Uncommon bull's head; steel and wood; brass collar; distinct eye and curled horn both sides of head; top point projection to pry off inset lid; bottom blade is one-edge sharp can opener. 6"L., $55.00.

Skillet

Cast iron; from Wagner Ware, Sidney, Ohio., $40.00.

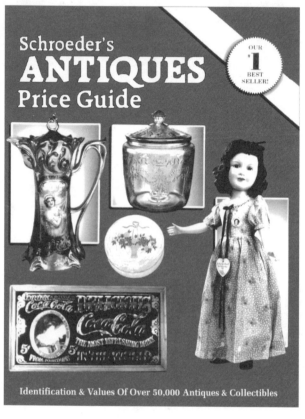